Dear Lee,

I will always be grateful
to you and Maruh for your
care and support of Sheila
and me. Thank you.

~ Thaer and Sheila Abdallah

2/13/21

Sheila

# SONG
## *in the*
# DESERT

*My journey from Baghdad to Boston*

Thaer Abdallah

AuthorHouse™
1663 Liberty Drive
Bloomington, IN 47403
www.authorhouse.com
Phone: 1 (833) 262-8899

This book is printed on acid-free paper.

ISBN: 978-1-7283-6790-3 (sc)
ISBN: 978-1-7283-6789-7 (e)

Library of Congress Control Number: 2020913188

Print information available on the last page.

Published by AuthorHouse 09/17/2020

authorHOUSE®

# INTRODUCTION

## Dedication

I want to dedicate this work to the ones who sacrificed so we could live, who went hungry so we could eat, and who lost sleep so we could rest peacefully. I also would like to dedicate this book to the beloved souls of my mother and father with much love, thanks and appreciation.

# TABLE OF CONTENTS

# CHAPTER ONE
# Memories of My Childhood in Baghdad

We always feel nostalgic for our own childhood. It is the most beautiful time of life and has some of the most beautiful moments. I have many memories that I have not forgotten. Those moments of my boyhood dreams and the ambitions of my youth were embroidered with childhood innocence. I will always remember the neighborhood where I lived that held all my childhood concerns, my happiness and every single detail of both pain and joy. This neighborhood contained all the episodes of my past. Ah, my old home! How I wish that those past days could come back … just to live another day in that warmth when I was a little child, so free of worries and stress.

I was born on February 8, 1970 on the eastern side of Al-Karrada, a popular area in Baghdad, Iraq, well-known for its classic alleyways, beautiful markets and kind and welcoming people. Despite the difficulties of life at that time, I have not forgotten those days.

My mother and siblings told me that I was born surrounded by a caul – the amniotic membrane, in the Palestinian dialect called, *Al-borns*. In our prevailing religious and cultural traditions, we believe that someone born covered in this kind of membrane has a special destiny, good luck and good fortune. This caused the nurse to steal this membrane, as she believed it would bring good luck and good fortune to the one who owned it. Next, a funny thing happened once we arrived home. An argument started between my family and my grandmother over who would be the first to name me. My grandmother wanted to name me Saeed ("happy"), and the rest of the family wanted the name Thaer ("rebel"). Finally, they agreed on Thaer as the official name, but I was still called Saeed at home to satisfy my grandma.

Despite my "happy" name and auspicious beginnings, I was also born under a political shadow. My parents were Palestinian, meaning that I was forever isolated as part of a community set apart. We Palestinians were an ethnic minority within Iraq. We were *in* Iraq but were never seen as *of* Iraq. The Iraqi government deliberately did not let us assimilate. My parents had fled their village in Haifa as children when Israeli bombers destroyed their homes. They and their parents and neighbors endured arduous journeys but wound up eventually in Iraq where they settled but were never fully welcomed. Palestinians in Iraq, and their children and descendants, never received citizenship. I was born in Iraq, but I am not Iraqi and from very early on I knew this. We had no citizenship, no right to own a home or land, no right to serve in a governmental office, and no right to even marry an Iraqi without permission. We had no passports, only Palestinian travel documents. We had to renew our residency cards regularly. This, for someone born in Iraq! The Iraqi government, and all the Arab governments, did this so that Palestinians would never feel comfortable and would want to return to Palestine. The Arab governments wanted to force the "Right to Return" movement. We were different from our neighbor Iraqis.

You will see that later in my life, this difference became deadly. But as a child, all I knew was that we Palestinians had our own dialect, neighborhoods, and customs. And in those days, the differences didn't seem to matter. Many of our neighbors were from various Iraqi sects -- Christians, Sunni, Shiite, Mandaeans -- and we all got alone very well. I will never forget the good times that we spent with these Iraqi families. We never thought about sectarian titles. We used to join in each other's feasts and festivals and visited each other all the time. Differences were never a matter of concern, as we were all like one body and lived in one intertwined family. We lived in peace, love and mercy. Life was full of joy, with an innocent feeling of simplicity flowing over it all.

These memories and events from my childhood in Al-Karrada that I'm going to narrate are from age 7 to 11 years old. We lived in a simple house located in a humble neighborhood called Al-Attar Street.

Ours was a small apartment that was part of a bigger building called Al-Hoash. It consisted of seven rooms, with each family living in one room. We were eight to ten families with relatives and nonrelatives all living together. Each family consisted of an average of six to eight members totaling about 60 people in the building. After my grandfather died, our grandma Khariah, who was my father's mother, lived with us. She was of Lebanese origin. We all lived in that one room that we used to call *serdap*, which means the basement.

I remember that my grandma used to sell sunflower seeds for a living from the big house. My father and I would roast the sunflower seeds using a metal bowl, called a *saj*, with a small fire beneath it to give the seeds a special flavor. Then we removed the paper covers from old books, shaped them into cones and filled them with the seeds for my grandma to sell.

We lived for about thirteen years in that house that had only one bathroom. That made me and my little brothers and sisters compete, running out to the bathroom after the end of a cartoon or movie we were watching. Sometimes we made a line at the bathroom door, each waiting for his or her turn. That made my father decide to build another kitchen and bathroom next to our room. I remember we all helped my father to build it. We were a big family of seven girls and six boys, and I was the tenth.

The days passed quickly without my being aware of the passage of time. Some of my brothers and sisters got married and I started going to school alone. My school was called Eastern Karrada School and it was a five-minute walk from my home. I never felt tired or bored because the way was full of tall green palm trees on the side of the road, the air was refreshing and the view from there was gorgeous. But the most amazing thing was my mother's breakfast. She would prepare the food while we were gathered around the circular table, excited and waiting for the meal that is called *fatah* in the Palestinian dialect. It is made of crumbled bread, sugar and cheese, all covered with tea or milk.

There was a small window overlooking our neighbor's room. My brother Thamer and I used to sit next to that window watching the neighbor's black and white TV. At that time, I was 8 years old and Thamer was 13, and we fought a little for the best view, but we shared the window. I remember that we watched Star Trek almost every day.

My father was a wonderful, kind and generous man. He bought us everything we asked for, meeting our desires for food, clothing and toys. He worked as a bus driver for the public double-decker bus called *Alamana tabkeen* in the Iraqi dialect. My father was honest and worked with so much energy. He also worked as a truck driver, carrying construction materials from Al-Mahmudiyah to the capital, Baghdad. My father's boss was an Iraqi man who trusted him to do a lot of deliveries for his business.

My father started to teach my brothers Thamer and Jamal the business of truck driving. Then Jamal worked with my dad. I can never forget the times when my dad came home carrying the family supplies of food, school bags and rain boots for winter. We used to compete, racing to open the door for him when he arrived. My father would cut wood to heat the room so that we would feel warm and able to sleep at night. We had a small hole open in the roof in order to get rid of the smoke. One day it was so windy that a neighbor's huge palm tree collapsed. My father took advantage of that and cut its wood into pieces and brought them home to use for heat. That made my mother very angry because it formed grime on the walls. She wanted them to be clean and white.

At the beginning of summer, we would sleep on the roof of the house. I remember that before the sunset my mother and my sisters went up to the roof to spill water on the roof to clean the dust and to cool it from the heat of the sun and to prepare it for the evening. When the evening came my mother brought floor mats and spread them out while everybody in the house took his own mattress to the roof placing them side-by-side. We also put curtains on the walls with ropes and nails as barriers between us and our neighbors. Everyone was respectful, moral and honorable. We felt like a big family in al-Hoash and shared many times of happiness and sadness together. On the roof my father kept a huge pot called *al-heb* made of clay with a small metal bowl inside that kept the water cold in the summer. If we felt thirsty at night, we could get a drink of pure cold water.

My brothers Thamer, Amer and I had wonderful times on the roof. My cousins used to come from Jordan to spend the summer holidays with us, so we boys would sleep on the roof, thrilled by the quiet nights and the moonlight and the beauty of the bright sky laden with shining stars. There was a nightclub two streets away from our house. Despite the distance, we were able to hear the traditional Iraqi songs accompanied by wonderful music because the nights were so quiet. I can still hear the branches of the trees in the dark swaying in the breeze. I had no sense of fear, when I looked down at my father who was sitting outside the house listening to the radio with our lovely German Shepherd named Fox beside him. My father was wearing his olive-green jacket that he had kept after the many days of the revolution against the English mandate in Palestine. When he was only fifteen, he spent two years in jail for smuggling weapons to the revolutionaries. My father also had a hunting rifle, and a large fishing net which he cast from a public bridge every Friday. Also, in Al-Karrada, I remember July 17th which was an Iraqi national day when people celebrated with fireworks that lit up the Baghdad sky. We ran to the roof to see those bright lights.

Behind our home there was a big yard where my father raised domestic animals such as rabbits, chickens and sheep and there were red and yellow fig trees and red and white berries. One day an incident occurred. While my grandma was hanging clothes on a rope a big sheep rushed towards her from behind and butted her. Because I witnessed that my father asked me to act like the sheep to show what happened. I performed that role so perfectly that it made every member of my family laugh. Even my father laughed out loud.

Our neighbors had a back yard full of fruit trees. There was a *narenj* tree with fruit that looks like an orange from the outside but has a sour taste like a lemon. We used to climb the tree to pick the fruit. It had a very delicious flavor, especially with soup in the winter. We also climbed a palm tree to get the dates. One day I fell down and had a lot of bruises, but I didn't give up. I kept trying again and again until I succeeded. I also climbed a huge, tall tree called the *ziziphus* tree, or *nabaq* in the Iraqi dialect. My cousins started to throw stones at the tree to knock down the cherries that they collected in bags despite the thorns in the branches.

One day, my aunt yelled at us to stop climbing the trees but we weren't listening to her. She brought a hose and hit my brother Thamer and me on our behinds and kept us inside her room for a few hours as a punishment for climbing the trees. Then we began to cry and begged her to open the door and let us out. She refused until we made a promise not to do that again. But of course, we did not keep the promise and kept climbing, over and over again. That back garden became like a family meeting place. The men and women talked about work, told jokes and laughed while drinking tea with cinnamon and eating cake with dates and fruit. Meanwhile, the kids played and picked fruit from the trees. We used this garden as a place to celebrate weddings, happy occasions and parties. Our relatives would come three days earlier to help prepare the sweets and pies.

My mother was interested in teaching my sisters how to cook, but the big burden of managing the household was on her since she loved to do everything herself including washing clothes and dishes, cooking and cleaning. To me, everything seemed simple and nice, smooth and spontaneous. At the feasts, *Eid* in Arabic, my mom arranged our clothes to make us look good, decent enough to meet our relatives when they came to our home or when we went to visit them.

I won't forget the games that we used to play with the children in the neighborhood. They were popular games in Baghdad called, *Shantr Bulbul* (like stickball), *Da'abl* (like marbles) and *Siphon* (like a mix of bowling and cricket). What fantastic days, full of joy and fun! I remember the car that sprayed white smoke to clear the air from insects. All the kids went running after that car as if we were birds floating above the clouds until we got into the heavy smoke and started coughing.

To keep my little brother and I at the house and prevent us from going out and causing trouble for my mother, my father came up with a great idea. He made us a swing from an old car roof rack that my brothers and my cousins happily played on. One day I was playing in the garden and digging in the ground. I found a small white bag. When I opened it, I found coins inside. I will never forget this incident. I still remember it very clearly.

When I was young, I was ambitious and had a lot of goals and dreams, to be a great artist and have a gallery. I loved painting and went to see art exhibits and the museums. I stood staring in front of the paintings for hours looking carefully at every single detail. I was inspired by them. This happened to me when I saw the work of all the great painters. It was all in God's hands, but I prayed I would achieve my goal one day, to paint, to share my feelings through art. There is no despair in life for those of us who want to grow and improve ourselves.

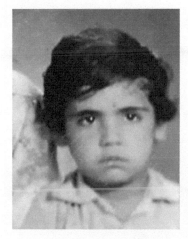

A photo of me when I was 5 years old

A sketch of my brother Thamer and I as we looked out the window to our neighbors' house to watch Star Trek on the television.

A photo of my brother Thamer and me

Thamer

An oil painting of my
neighborhood back in 1975

Iraqi bread

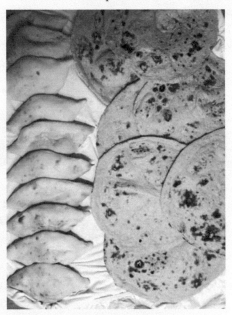

A view from Abu Nawas

# CHAPTER TWO
# Al-Baladiyat during the Iran-Iraq War

Everyone has memories that we never forget. Because of their special glow, we may think about them every day. This is about missing a past that is gone and will never come back. Today I have almost forgotten the feelings the past gave me, such as the wonderful moments I experienced in Al-Karrada and those that I also felt in many other places.

In this chapter I will share my memories from Al-Baladiyat, the neighborhood we lived in after we left Al-Karrada. During that time my father was working hard to improve our daily lives. An apartment was an essential thing that the family needed to have in order to live a better life. My father applied for an apartment in a complex of buildings located in Al-Baladiyat. They were built especially for the Palestinian refugees in Iraq who had emigrated from Palestine after 1948 during the era of the former Iraqi President, Ahmed Hassan Al-Baker. Former president Al-Baker ruled Iraq from 1968-1979.

After only a few days of waiting for a decision, the agency that worked for the Ministry of Social Affairs informed us that we had an apartment. It was a big apartment on the first floor that had two bedrooms, a living room, kitchen, bathroom and a balcony that faced the street and had a beautiful view. The complex consisted of about 17 buildings. Each building had four entrances with each entrance leading to three floors. Each floor contained four apartments, some small and others quite big. Once we had the keys to our new apartment and although our lives improved in this bigger and better home, we had mixed feelings that we never had before, feelings of happiness and sadness at the same time. We felt the joy of having a large and great-looking apartment, but at the same time, the sadness of leaving Al-Karrada. We were leaving the friends and neighbors with whom we had spent wonderful times and we carried their memory with us, saving images of them in our hearts. In the innocence and wonder of childhood, I had spent so many amazing times there. Those are days that I will never, ever forget.

We moved to Al-Baladiyat in 1980. My mother and my sisters moved first to clean the apartment, dust it and prepare it and then we followed with the luggage and furniture. I remember new feelings of delight as we settled in, placing the furniture and decorating the apartment. My father asked my brothers and I to sleep in the living room and my sisters to sleep in one of the bedrooms, while my parents slept in the other bedroom.

We started to meet people as we adapted and socialized with our new neighbors. It was a big complex of buildings, and all our neighbors were Palestinian refugees who had emigrated to Iraq from Palestine because of the war in 1948. They were originally from villages in and around Haifa like Ejzem and Ain Kazal, and they believed they would be allowed to return after the war. Of course, they were never allowed to return.

One time when I went with my brothers Thamer and Amer to eat falafel sandwiches at an Iraqi restaurant, we suddenly heard screaming inside the restaurant. We looked up and saw the owner crying because he heard the news that the former president, Ahmed Hassan Al-Baker, had died. At that time the current president was Saddam Hussein who had been the vice president and was assigned the presidency after the resignation of Al-Baker in 1979.

At the time, this meant nothing to me. I didn't think about politics as a child. Later, as a teen and young adult, I decided I did not care for Saddam Hussein. He was a bully and a dictator who robbed my community as well as other Iraqi communities of their freedoms and rights. Like many teens, I had a strong sense of justice. I refused to join the Baath Party, and as a result I never went to college, because college was funded by the government only for party members. But on that day when the former president had died, I was not even thinking about politics. I was too busy focused on school, studies, friends, and family.

I remember helping my brothers transfer our profiles from our old school in Al-Karrada to the new school in Al-Baladiyat. Its name was Ramallah Elementary School. The school was located on Al-Mashtal Street and was close to our home. The government ordered that meals be given to all the students in the schools at that time, so during the break between classes we enjoyed free meals that included milk, cheese, bread, eggs and cookies. The vice principal was Palestinian so we felt we would be treated fairly.

The school had gardens full of trees where we could find a lot of birds. My cousin Ahmed used to make traps to catch doves and pigeons in the trees. After school, we would go with him to get the traps and went back to school without telling our parents.

We started to build more friendships with families in the neighborhood and I went with my parents to visit them. We became very close to them. My best friend was a boy named Esam. He lived near my home. We would sit together on a bench made of concrete that my father had built for us, staying together until after midnight laughing and telling jokes. We had a lot of fun together. My brothers and I played soccer with the neighbors on the street in front of our apartment. There were also large black pipes under the ground that we hid behind when we played hide and seek. We played a lot of games. We also had fights with the Iraqi kids who lived close to our complex. Our clothes were dirty, and we were tired and exhausted when we got back home. It was very stupid to do that. Now I would wish to meet them again and become friends with them.

When I turned twelve, I went to the Al-Awda Middle School that was also in Al-Baladiyat. The name Al-Awda means "the return" so it was designed to make us want to return to Palestine. My mother used to wake up early to make breakfast and prepare our clothes, then she woke us up to eat and prepare for school. We were so lazy getting out of the bed. Carrying our books, we walked to school with the other kids in the neighborhood. In the winter after school the boys and I used to gather in one of our homes to play. One time we played at Kamal's house and another time in Ayad's. On our way home, we stopped at a store to buy candy, cookies and biscuits. That year, my father also helped me to buy a bike. The brand was an Indian Twenty-Eight and the color was green. I loved riding all around the neighborhood and it gave me a sense of freedom and adventure.

The weeks fell into a comfortable pattern. When I was 14 or 15, every Thursday my mother and my brother Tariq and I would taxi to visit her mother, Aisha, about 40 minutes away. We would stay overnight with them. My grandmother lived in three rooms with her daughter Mariam and Mariam's six children. Every Friday my cousin Khatab and I went to the movies in a downtown Baghdad theater. Many of the movies from India were very sad, and sometimes I cried, but other times I was happy. Sometimes there were English movies with Arabic subtitles. All told there were nine movie theatres in Baghdad, and I visited them all! We spent many happy Friday afternoons in the magical darkness of the movies. And afterwards, when we stepped out of the darkness of the movie house, we were struck by the blinding sun and warmth. I remember wandering the streets for hours in that enveloping warmth, with a feeling of freedom and happiness.

On Thursday and Friday evenings when we gathered as a family, the kids all stayed up late because we didn't have school the next day. My father bought a color television set for the family and I still remember the shows we enjoyed together: Sindbad cartoons, Children's Cinema, Children's Art Studio, Sports of the Week, Bud Spencer, and a science program in which an elderly man, Kamil Al Debaugh, taught the audience about geology, biology, and so many interesting topics.

My dad thought of starting a small project to improve the income for our family. Because the complex did not have any stores and the residents needed to buy their daily supplies, my dad opened a store. He sold candy, biscuits and soft drinks including Coca Cola, Pepsi, Sinalco and Seven-Up, as well as household products and cleaning supplies. It was the first store in the complex. Those were beautiful days for me. Words cannot describe the feelings of happiness and satisfaction that we experienced. Everything seemed so simple and wonderful.

In the beginning, my parents used to wake us up early in the morning to help them carry the heavy boxes of soft drinks. Then my dad bought an old Volkswagen for shopping and carrying the heavy goods, and to use as a taxi. After that our financial situation became much better. And my family became bigger too. Some of my brothers moved to other places because they got married and started their own families. But they always visited us every Friday. My brother Ali lived in Al-Zafarania and my brother Jamal lived in Al-Karrada close to our old home. Ali worked as a manager for a British company called Metro Baghdad because he was fluent in English. Jamal worked as a driver for the British Academy in Baghdad. We visited each other often even without special occasions. We drank tea and coffee and talked about life. Our connection was tight, and we stayed very close to each other.

These times seemed to me to be easy and peaceful. My brother Ali used to organize trips for us with our relatives. He took us to many amazing places like Salman Park, Al-Tharthar lake, which is situated northwest of Baghdad between the Tigris and the Euphrates rivers, and to Al-Habbaniyah lake located west of Baghdad. Each family brought homemade food, drinks and sweets. In the summertime, my uncle, Abu Sameer, and my father's cousin, Abu Isaac, visited us from Jordan during school vacations. Abu Isaac had earned the black belt in karate, so he would train me and Thamer in some of the karate movements and techniques. We all spent lovely times together. But nothing stays the same, and even these beautiful moments started to disappear.

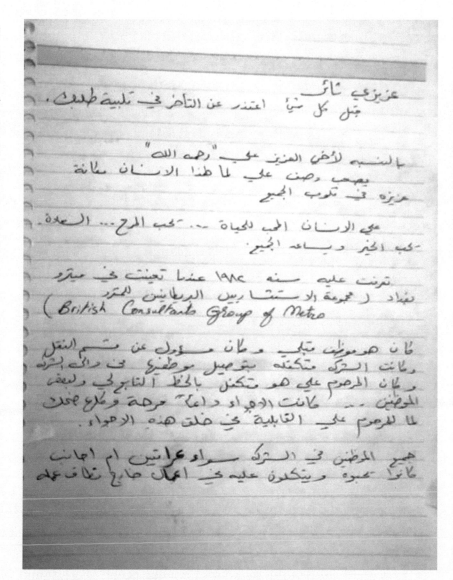

Vera Ohanian wrote this letter about my brother talking about how he is loved by everyone in his company

In September of 1980 everything changed. Because of a conflict on the border between Iraq and Iran, a war started between these two countries. We heard the warning sirens and the sounds of bombing on our way to school, and we saw Iranian rockets falling on many areas of Baghdad. Every time we heard the sirens at night we rushed to bunkers and special shelters made of concrete, following the instructions of the civil defense organization. We were very careful about going near objects on the road, even toys or candy, because they might be explosives placed by mercenaries working for the Iranians. Because of that a lot of young people died in this war. The war became more serious between the Iraqis and Iranians, so the Iraqi government pressured the Palestinians in Iraq to participate in the war. We were neutral but we were forced to fight with Iraq or face deportation. Palestinians died alongside Iraqis in this war until it ended on August 8, 1988.

During those difficult years, my hobby of painting began to grow and evolve, and my talent developed by drawing maps and illustrative drawings for my biology class. I joined the Al-Baladiyat Palestinian Youth Organization that met about a half hour's walking distance from home. They had many programs such as Palestinian folk dancing, called Dabke, painting, singing and music, so we learned a lot there. There was a man named Khalid (may he rest in peace), who taught me drawing skills. Another man, Taki, also provided us with art materials. I participated in many other activities including poetry, sports and entertainment. We wore uniforms and even went camping during summer vacation.

I painted portraits of my friends and neighbors and drew maps and illustrations for school. My neighbor Kamal and I used to work together on calligraphy and painting. My first exhibition was in Algeria when I was only 15 years old. By high school, I became increasingly drawn to painting and so my dream and my ambition grew. My uncle Jamal was a carpenter, and I made frames for drawings in his workshop and spread oil on a piece of canvas. I waited for the oil to dry then I started drawing on it. When I couldn't find a good piece of canvas, I cut a type of canvas called *Al-Hmayoun* that was in my mother's closet, without telling her. Sometimes she got very angry at this behavior. My father often stood next to me watching me draw and encouraging me to develop my skills. I once drew my father's portrait on a piece of wood called *Al-Veiberh*.

It occurred to me to draw a lot of famous people. For example, I drew the actor Bruce Lee and two Palestinian leaders, Abu Ammar and Abu Jihad, on plates using pencil and charcoal. I copied large pictures and small ones. I copied a famous painting of a crying baby using oil paint brushes. As my skills grew, my dreams grew. I promised myself to make my very best effort to learn the art of painting in Italy someday, but I was not able to achieve that dream.

I have many memories of school. I remember very clearly the principal, vice principal, and teachers of math, physics, biology, and religion. I remember in particular the religion teacher who was a Palestinian and was blind. Every Thursday we had a morning assembly. We all stood together while they raised the Iraqi flag and we sang the Iraqi National Anthem. I also remember that I used to be a very fast runner.

Some of the teachers used to hit our hands with a thick stick of wood in the cold weather if we forgot to do our homework or came late to school. There was one teacher who always seemed nervous and was frightening. Everyone was afraid of her. Many students didn't like her because she hit them harshly. Once she asked a student sitting in front of me a question and he did not know the answer. She beat him severely and then she asked me. I also didn't know the answer and she came slowly from behind me and tried to hit me with a book, but I put my head down quickly and made the book fall out of her hands. She tried to hit me again, but she failed. I could not tolerate this aggressive behavior, so I pushed her and yelled at her, "Why do you want to hit me? Who do you think you are that you can do that to us?" She went out of the classroom to the principal's office.

The vice principal was very kind. She also knew all the students because she taught us geography. She talked to me about what happened. I said to her, "Why does my teacher want to beat us so badly in this very cold weather?" I was crying with tears running down my cheeks. I told the vice principal that I would leave the school and never come back. She went to the teacher and yelled at her. Then the principal announced a meeting to inform the teachers that beating the students was forbidden and uncivilized. The school stood on the side of the students which was a great help. The other students told me that they were very happy about what I had done. I met with the social workers in school several times and later I visited the vice principal after graduation because I heard that she had become the principal.

Sometimes when I look back, I see those daily conflicts with school and family as just extensions of the larger war with Iran, whose endless mortars and sirens broke our peace every day. The large and the small are one and the same thing. It was as if the war had poisoned not only the relationship between our countries, but the relationships among families and friends, fraying the fabric that held us together. In those days, there was a lot of conflict in my home. While my brothers and sisters and I continued to have adventures together and enjoy pranks and games, all too often we and my parents were fighting. My brother Jamal and his wife were not getting along, and he started drinking too much. I was a teenager and I argued with my father a lot in those days. Sometimes my parents also fought. The economy was terrible and daily expenses piled up, causing stress. One day, my parents were fighting, and I thought my father would hit my mother. I stood in front of him and dared him to hit me instead. He wound up chasing me around the house, furious. This was not good for his heart and he suffered for it. To this day I feel regret when I remember those days and it is painful to write about it. I loved my father, and Jamal, and all my family. They were good people, but no one is perfect, and those years were very hard for all of us.

I moved to another school, the Al-Tadhya night school, so that I could work during the day with my brother Amer in a construction company. I gave the money to my parents to support the family. So I finished my high school education in a non-traditional way, apart from my longtime friends. It was lonely. After high school, I had hoped to go on to college to study art, but those dreams did not come true. I was stubborn and refused to join Saddam Hussein's Baath Party, so college was not an option for me without the aid of a government scholarship. I was not in a good place psychologically. Again, it was as if the war had poisoned my life from the inside, not just the outside. Little did I know at the time, even more conflict was about to begin.

"Memories": An oil painting of my second neighborhood Al-Baladiyat. This was an area of only Palestinians.

This is called a Soba. This was what my mother used as a stove to cook our food. It was also used as a heater to keep the house warm.

# CHAPTER THREE
# The First Losses in My life

In 1988, after a bitter conflict and a difficult time for all of us, the war ended between Iraq and Iran. It ended by a decision of the Security Council at the United Nations. This war left many victims on both sides numbering approximately one million dead, injured or missing. Right after the declaration of the end of the war Iraqis started celebrating the peace. Spontaneously people started setting off displays of fireworks in the air as a way of expressing their happiness. Both Iran and Iraq considered themselves the winner in this war despite the losses on both sides.

At the end of the eighties, after the war, my older brother Ali (may he rest in peace) started to organize tours for my family and my relatives to archaeological sites and tourist destinations every month that pleased all of us. We prepared for these trips by cooking food and buying beverages and packing things for entertainment such as footballs, tennis rackets, dominos and backgammon. Like in the old days we went to lake Al-Tharthar and Al-Habbaniyah where we swam in the lake, organized races and ate delicious food. We had a wonderful time. Around this time, my father drove a Toyota as a taxi for a Mitsubishi manager, who was often welcomed into our home to enjoy delicious Arabic food.

But at the same time, my father was diagnosed with heart disease and asthma. His health became worse until he completely collapsed. Despite his severe illness, he continued to work hard, challenging the disease and the cold weather. He had a hobby of collecting scrap metal and fixing it so that he could sell it or use it later. One day he was fixing it in our garden at home to bring it back to work again and fell very ill. We had to take him to the Ibn al-Nafees hospital close to Al-Andalus Square in Al-Karrada in Baghdad. We all went together to stay with him at the hospital. For a long time, my brothers and I helped him by alternating taking him every two or three days to the hospital to receive treatment that included administering a nasal spray for asthma and also IV fluids. But he never got better, and he passed away the same year.

I was very young at that time, just 17 years old. I was working with my brother-in-law as a carpenter in a company called British Metro Consultants in Al-Mansour. While I was walking home one day, in the distance I noticed a tent in front of our house. Traditionally, a large tent was set up when someone had died, so that all who came to pay their respects would be sheltered from the hot sun. A little girl came up to me and said, "Do you know who this condolence is for?"

"No. Who is it for?" I asked.

She said, "Your father died today, I'm sorry for that."

I did not believe the news that my father had died. It was a sudden and huge shock and it left a big, deep wound inside me. It was a very difficult moment and I started to cry. I felt so sad for this loss that I did not go home that day. I refused to believe this bad news or face the painful reality. I felt a sudden emptiness in my life. I especially remember the early morning the day before his death. He came to our bedroom to put pillows under our heads and made sure that we had blankets on so we wouldn't feel cold. It was as if he was aware that day that his spirit would soon be delivered to his God.

We buried my father in the cemetery of Imam Al-Ghazali at Bab Al-shek in Baghdad. Even now that wound has not healed. Then things got worse. Destiny knocked on our door again with the death of my elder brother Ali in a car accident. His car overturned near the General Directorate of Security building close to our home. I received the news through a call from my brother-in-law, Abu Bashir. He spoke to me in a calm voice in order not to shock me explaining that my brother had had a car accident. This was a bitter tragedy and a great shock to me and my family. I began to run madly towards the direction of the incident ten minutes away from my home. As I got closer to the place of the accident, I felt more and more pain and grief. I felt my chest tighten and my heart twist.

When I saw the scene of the overturned car and the people gathered around it, I quickly asked, "Where is my brother?" They said that he was taken to the Al-Kindy hospital on Al-Thawra Street. I rushed to get a taxi to go to the hospital. Once there, I saw my brother lying on the bed. He was already dead. I left the room and went to the corridor alone and started to cry. At the same time, two police officers walked by with a handcuffed man. I thought that this person had caused my brother's accident and I ran toward him and hit him in the back. But I was mistaken and confused. I then waited with my brother's body a long time until I reached a moment when I could not tolerate being at the hospital beside him without being able to help him. I went back to the house. None of us could believe that painful news. My brother Ali was like another father to us. He was the eldest. He was the candle that lit up the house. He was the backbone of the family.

We had his condolences in our house. He had many friends from all over the country who came to the house along with our many relatives, neighbors and his co-workers from the British company where he worked. Our house was full of people crying. No one could believe what had happened.

After that, I worked with my brothers Thamer and Amer, opening my father's store in the mornings and continuing my high school education at night school. Things were never really the same in our family after that year, when we lost both our father and our brother.

# CHAPTER FOUR
# The First Invasion of Iraq

In August 1990, another war started. Saddam Hussein directed Iraqi soldiers to invade Kuwait. He had said that Kuwait was stealing Iraqi oil. I felt sad when this war started, because I knew that the Palestinians in Kuwait would suffer, because the Palestinian leader Yasser Arafat had come out in support of Saddam Hussein. I also became worried as the months wore on, that the United States and other countries would enter the war, against Iraq. I felt that we had just escaped the bombs and terror of the Iran-Iraq war, and I could not bear that it would all start over again.

At first the war was only in Kuwait. We heard from our neighbors that many Iraqi people joined the soldiers in Kuwait to steal from the Kuwaiti people – cars, gold, paintings. The United Nations and the United States told Saddam Hussein many times to stop, but he did not stop. On the news, we were shown maps about how Kuwait was supposed to be part of Iraq and that it belonged to us. Months passed, and the United States president George H. W. Bush gave Iraq one last chance to withdraw before carrying out a military attack. But Saddam Hussein did not comply with United Nations Security Council resolutions and he threatened to bomb Israel. After the deadline passed, the United States carried out airstrikes in Baghdad and other areas. They targeted not only military bases but infrastructure, like bridges, electric plants, and water treatment plants. They made sure that Iraq would be crippled for years to come.

The actual bombing was unlike anything I had ever experienced, even during the war with Iran. It felt like the end of the world. Many of my family members, including my sisters and brothers with their spouses and children, all gathered in one apartment. When we heard the sirens sound, we quickly extinguished our candles for fear that we would be targeted. We wondered if we would see the next day. The ground shook with the force of the bombs and the night sky lit up like daytime. But believe it or not, when this happened night after night without end, we got used to it. Sometimes we and our neighbors gathered at night, women, men, and children all gathering in their own groups. Each had their own way to fill the void of boredom and terror: men played cards and dominoes, women told stories of the past, and children played with whatever they could find.

The nights were long. The days became longer, as we started feeling the crisis from lack of gasoline, water, electricity, food, and supplies. Merchants began hoarding their goods, and long lines formed at gas stations and bakeries. At night, the electricity cut out, so we had no way to hear the news except to know by sound which neighborhoods were being bombed. My brother Jamal decided to rig up the battery of his car to the radio and TV, so we could watch and hear the news. We listened to "Voice of Free Iraq" which broadcast from Prague and covered events in Iraq, as well as some Arab stations.

Through the radio, we heard that life was difficult all over Iraq. There was no gasoline for cars and the roads were destroyed. It was almost impossible to get clean water or food during that time. We were still shocked that the war had happened at all, and that the situation was getting worse. People were so panicked and scared. They couldn't believe what was happening.

Thankfully, the bombing lasted only about one month. The Iraqi army ran away, for the most part. But even though they were running away, the American fighters still slaughtered them. At least 10,000 died fleeing along the Highway of Death in Basra in the south.

But the real war would last much, much longer. A few days after the end of the war, the United Nations Security Council imposed economic sanctions to meet the demands made by the United States to the Security Council. These sanctions were among the most severe sanctions in the world, and they continued for thirteen years. This decision had negative effects on everybody in Iraq. It led to a significant imbalance and deterioration in the economy, affecting the infrastructure, agriculture and industry throughout the country.

Also, because the sanctions prevented Iraq from importing anything from many countries, it led to a decrease in medicine and the medical devices and services that every hospital needed to treat patients. Therefore, the health of the people was compromised. This led to the deaths of more than 500,000 children as a result of hunger and the lack of emergency medicine and the most basic requirements for life.

Gradually life deteriorated as things got worse and worse, including standards of behavior. Trust diminished, and fraud and cheating became common. People had to take all sorts of twisted and convoluted paths just to survive and live their lives. The strong preyed on the weak, and the weak had no place in what had become of society. Everything was collapsing, which seemed to be what was intended by those who decided to hurt Iraq and her people. I was no different from everyone else, struggling to endure in order to earn a living and keep what I had. However, I was determined to stay committed to the standards of morality and behavior that my parents had taught me. For this reason, I continued to work night and day in different jobs. I divided my time between working early in the morning in a restaurant, a job in a contracting company and helping my older brother sell cigarettes in Al-Kifah Street in Baghdad. I also helped my other siblings with their businesses that included a small shop.

Later two of my sisters married Jordanian men and went to Jordan with their husbands and settled there. Not long after this, in 1993, my sister got me a visa to come to Jordan. There was a Jordanian ruling preventing Palestinians from staying in Amman for more than three months, but three months was better than nothing. While there I had the opportunity to work as an artist and I drew a portrait of Princess Haya. I gave it to her as a gift when she came to Amman International Stadium. She liked it! After the three months, I packed my bags to return to Baghdad as it was never far from my mind, despite the bad situation there.

In 1996 I got another visa to go to Jordan. I overstayed that visa and remained there for a year. I worked secretly and illegally with one of my cousins in a café. I worked there from 9 a.m. to 9 p.m. for one year until I became ill with a stomach ulcer that caused me a great deal of pain. I couldn't have an operation there because I had overstayed my residency in Jordan. (The king later issued a royal pardon to people who had overstayed their visas). I decided to go to Baghdad to have the operation so I could be close to my family. Before I said goodbye to the café owner and my friends, the owner came to see me. He gave me a sum of money made up from donations for me from people in the community. I thanked him profusely. This money had come at exactly the right time. I returned to Baghdad and after undergoing various medical tests, the doctor decided I should have the operation the next day in Al-Rahibat Hospital in Baghdad. Due to the care and competence of the excellent nurses, the operation was successful. I stayed in the hospital for five days under the care and observation of the doctors. After I recovered, my mother (God rest her soul) visited as well as my brothers, sisters, aunts and friends. I had pain at the site of the surgery for at least three months afterwards.

Meanwhile, Iraq was deteriorating even further. It had been almost six years, but the sanctions still had not been lifted and the Iraqi economy was in a state of total collapse. There was no hope that the Security Council would cancel the sanctions. The factories, refineries, generating station and even the sanitation system were destroyed. Nothing functioned. Because of unemployment and the lack of money, people were forced into theft and fraud and cheating. These were things we had never encountered before. In the past, we used to leave the doors unlocked without worrying that somebody could go in and steal the house or the car.

Due to this difficult living situation in the country during these years, I could not satisfy my dream to enter the Institute of Fine Arts, so I made a most difficult decision for a brighter future. I chose to travel outside Iraq in the hopes that I could find a better life. I planned to go to Turkey, because as a Palestinian I was not able to enter Jordan. I planned to go first to northern Iraq into the Kurdistan area and then from Iraq into Turkey. In order to enter northern Iraq, I had to go around Iraqi checkpoints.

I went to the northwest side of Mosul where there were Christian villages close to Kurdistan. It was dangerous because we were unable to travel to Kurdistan due to the problems between the Kurds and the Iraqi regime at that time. When I arrived at Al-Qush bordering Erbil I met a Christian family in the village, and I spent the night with them. The father introduced me to his son. They were very generous. The next day, the son took me to a village named Busan. We walked for four hours. It was rainy, windy and cold and the road was muddy. We reached a house belonging to a Yazidi family and I spent the night with them.

The next day, early in the morning, I hired a jeep. The driver took us between the hills and off the roads. It was dangerous and a long way until we finally arrived in Duhok City, in Kurdistan. A Kurdish family was waiting for me. They were very nice and welcoming people and their house was cozy. It was located behind a Kurdish radio station. They provided me with food and beverages. The house was in a very nice area between the mountains and was surrounded by trees and a wonderful natural environment. I stayed with them for a few days. They spoke Kurdish but they understood a little bit of Arabic too. I learned some Kurdish words from them. But I had to continue the journey to Turkey, so I thanked them for their hospitality and generosity, and I took a taxi to Zako, a town close to the Iraqi-Turkish border.

When I approached the Iraqi-Turkish border, a security patrol stopped me. They belonged to the Peshmerga, the military forces in the autonomous region of Iraqi Kurdistan. They arrested me and took me to a central Duhok jail where I stayed for a month without any investigation by the appropriate authorities. By chance, while I was sitting in the rest area with other prisoners, I heard the jailor ask who wanted to offer his time to clean the outer courtyard of the prison. I rushed to volunteer because I was bored and hoped to get some fresh air. They took me outside, and while I was cleaning there was a security guard standing near me, watching me. He asked me where I was from. I told him that I was Palestinian and then I told him the whole story.

After completing the cleaning, I heard one of the guards call out my name, so I went out and saw a man waiting for me. The police released me from jail. I found out later that the man was related to the Kurdish family who had hosted me at their home. I thanked him for his help.

In spite of my weak financial situation and the difficulties that I faced, I didn't give up and I decided to go to Erbil because I heard that there was a big chance that I could find someone who could help me to leave Iraq. I tried to find a way to travel to Turkey with a fake passport. One day I met a person who belonged to the Iraqi opposition against the Iraqi regime. He introduced me to one of his officials. That officer welcomed me and offered to help me. He asked me to give him my Palestinian travel document and he would give me an Iraqi passport. But I refused, I thanked him for the offer and left. I felt that giving up my Palestinian travel document would be giving up my personality. It wasn't worth it. I didn't have enough money to rent a room, so I had to spend the night outside on a mountain. It was a very hard time. The weather was cold, rainy, and windy, and there was thunder. I did not have enough cover to protect me from the biting cold. This bitter experience had not helped me achieve anything, so I decided to go back to Baghdad.

When I got back to Baghdad there were no jobs, and life was very difficult. My mother, my brothers Jamal, Amer and Thamer and I all fought to keep our little shop so we could continue to earn a living from it. My brothers Jamal and Thamer also sold cigarettes in the Al-Shorj neighborhood. In the year 2000 my brother Jamal became ill. A swollen gland appeared on his neck and the doctor decided to operate on it as it appeared to be infected. I went with him to the hospital in Al-Karrada where they performed the operation. Afterwards it was discovered that my brother had lung cancer and it had spread quickly. The doctors tried to defeat the disease with chemotherapy, but the cancer was eating away at his body. He went for treatment at Ibn Al-Nafees hospital. My brothers Thamer, Amer and Tariq stayed with him in shifts. Eventually, he could not sleep unless he was sitting up, and it was difficult for him to breathe. He remained in this state for three months. In 2002, he raised his hands up to us and then he died in front of our eyes. My grief and anger made me lose control. I felt as though my head was going to explode with rage and I broke a window with my bare hands. I started screaming in my pain and anguish of losing my beloved and kind brother Jamal who was as openhearted as a child and who always helped everyone. We held a funeral ceremony for him over three days. Our employer at the time, who owned the cigarette company and had loved Jamal very much, paid for the funeral expenses. This was another great loss for my mother and the family.

# CHAPTER FIVE
# The 2003 Invasion of Iraq

In April 2003, the people of Baghdad woke up to a tragedy that wounded their feelings of pride and dignity. We saw United States aircraft entering and bombing Baghdad, which fell without any resistance.

For many months leading up to this, we had heard reports on the news about the American government accusing Iraq of having chemical weapons. Every day, we heard reports about the United Nations inspectors. They checked everything, even the leaves on the trees! But George Bush had decided that he would start a war. Many human rights organizations sent people to Baghdad to protest and try to stop the war. Many peace activists risked their lives to prevent the bombing. We also saw on TV many peace demonstrations in the United States, so we knew that many Americans did not want the war.

I felt that they would succeed and that there would be no war. I felt that the American people were with us! So I cannot describe the pain I felt in my heart when the bombing started anyway. Each bomb was like a new wound in my heart.

The previous night, I had gone to my maternal grandfather's house in Al-Hurriya located in northwest Baghdad. I used to go to his home often because I missed talking to my uncles. They were like friends to me, especially my uncle Hassan, maybe because we are almost the same age.

That day, we were sitting in my grandfather's house listening to the news from the French radio station from Monte Carlo. The battery radio was the only way to get the news because the Iraqi government had cut the electricity. We heard that the Security Council was considering a decision made by the United States and a coalition to start military strikes against Iraq. We were not so sure, but we related the cut of our electricity with the possibility that it was to prevent the aircrafts from hitting their targets successfully.

At exactly two o'clock in the morning we started to hear sirens blaring everywhere as a warning sign of the beginning of war. Then explosions began, and we started to see columns of smoke rising from many areas. The coalition aircrafts were prowling the skies of Baghdad from the north and the south. They bombed all the electric power generation centers as well as bridges and water purification centers. Targeting these places destroyed the Iraqi infrastructure and the consequences of its effects still exist today, as people are still suffering from the need for electricity and pure water.

The next day, I decided to go back to my home in Al-Baladiyat. While I was heading to the downtown area called Bab Al-Sharqi to take the bus, I was stunned that all the public transportation was completely paralyzed. The streets were empty of people. Because everybody feared the bombing, they stayed home or went to the shelters to protect themselves from the rockets. So I had to walk home. Sometimes people gave me rides, but it still took many hours to get there.

During the bombing, my mother, my sisters, my brothers and their children all gathered together in our house. About 30 persons spread out in the kitchen, corridor and in the bedrooms. The sounds of the bombing intensified and came close to our home. We sat all together to pray and ask God with humbled and honest hearts to protect us from all harm. While we were praying, my niece Noora, who was 9 years old, was also praying with us. In all sincerity, and for reasons we could not understand, she said "God save Jamal Abdel Nasser!" who was the deceased former President of Egypt. Despite our fear and distraction, we all burst out laughing. We all still clearly remember that incident. Noora now lives as a refugee in New Zealand with my sister Hanan's family.

*Photo of when America invaded Iraq*

Every night the bombing intensified without stopping, and the fear and panic increased. We lost our water and electricity. There was no movement of people on the streets and the shops closed their doors. We started to run out of food. That was when my mother came up with a great idea that helped her to make bread for us. In the past, we would go to the corner bakery to buy fresh bread every day. But we were afraid to go out. So, my mother placed a big box of metal with holes on the top of it on the oil heater, made the dough for the bread and cooked it on the hot metal. It helped us to survive the war without going out and endangering our lives.

The Iraqi army disappeared, and some Iraqis even destroyed the statue of Saddam Hussein. They were cheering against him. But this sudden change put Iraq in a state of chaos and panic. We were shocked and felt great sadness for the fall of Baghdad.

One night, we heard bombs very close by, at the building near us where my sister Siham lived with her family. I heard people yelling that there was a fire. I was worried that the fire would spread. Everyone had canisters of gas that we used to power the stoves and I was worried that the fire would spread to where the gas was stored and cause terrible explosions. I called my nephew Riyad and said, "Come on, we have to go fight this fire!"

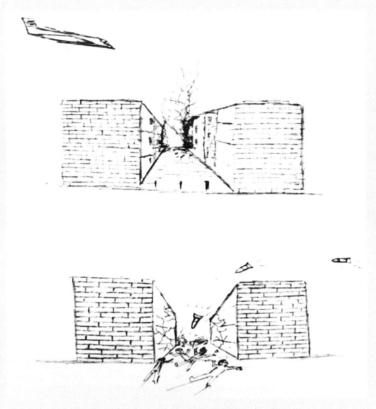

Illustration of the American planes dropping bombs in our neighborhood

We grabbed gallon bottles of water that we had set aside for emergency and ran to the fire. When we threw water on the fire, the fire hissed and the smoke got worse.

The Americans fired flares over the building. I thought they wanted to see who was there. We were worried that they would shoot us, so we ran into the building next door. Eventually we were able to put out the fire. I'll never forget the burning feeling of the smoke in my lungs. I could barely breathe.

Many days and nights of bombings continued. During the chaos, I felt deeply anxious and sad and thought a lot about the fate of the Palestinian refugees in Iraq and what would happen to them. The insecurity caused riots in the streets. The looting increased because the jails were opened and the prisoners escaped. I was worried about the safety of my community. I wanted to do something to protect my family and the rest of the Palestinians.

Let me explain why Palestinians were in so much danger. When Saddam was in power, he used to go on the TV and brag about how he supported Palestine, he supported Palestinians. The Iraqi people who suffered so much terror under Saddam thought that he gave us Palestinians free land, apartments, money, cars, everything. So they resented us. But the rumors were not true. Saddam just wanted to look like an Arab hero by saying he supported Palestine.

In reality, Saddam hurt the Palestinian people. Like I said before, in Iraq we had no rights. We had no Iraqi citizenship, even though most of us were born in Iraq. We had no right to own land, or a home, or a car, or even a phone. In order for us to obtain any of these things, an Iraqi citizen had to sign the papers. We had no right to hold government office or be part of the army. We had no right to marry an Iraqi citizen unless we got special permission. We had to register and re-register every few months with the Offices of Immigration and Residence – even though we were born in Iraq! These policies were all to isolate the Palestinian community and make us uncomfortable in Iraq, so that we would long for Palestine and push for the "Right of Return." In reality, Saddam sold us for a political purpose.

After the fall of the regime, many Iraqi gangs, mostly Shi'a, started targeting Palestinians, as a way of getting revenge for what they perceived as Saddam's favoritism to us, and our supposed support of Saddam. As you know, I never supported Saddam Hussein. I refused to join the Baath party. But whether or not any Palestinian had supported Saddam, life became very dangerous for us after the fall of the regime.

I was worried about the safety of the Palestinian community, even immediately after the invasion. For example, many of us were stuck without identity documents. As Palestinians in Iraq, we were issued identity documents by the Iraqi government. These documents had to be renewed every few years. We would bring our documents to the Offices of Immigration, pay a fee, then wait for a few weeks before we would return to pick up the new document. So anyone who had turned in documents in the months before the invasion was stuck without identity papers. I was worried that these crucial papers would get lost because militias were burning the government buildings and stealing from the banks and museums. So my friend Mahmoud and I decided to go to the Offices of Immigration and Residence for Palestinians for the purpose of collecting personal documents and papers pertaining to Palestinian refugees, just in case these documents were caught up in the wave of looting that extended everywhere.

Mahmoud had a Range Rover, so he was able to drive us there. When we arrived at the building, we didn't find anyone. It was very quiet, and there were no employees or security inside. We started to collect all the travel and identity documents and stamps and put them into two large bags. We went to the Palestinian compound in Al-Baladiyat and gave the documents that belonged to the Palestinians living there. They were very thankful and glad to have their documents. While distributing the travel documents, I accidentally found my sister's request for the renewal of her travel documents that she had submitted with an appointment to pick them up in April 2003. Due to the war and the chaos, she never received them. I had managed to get an official stamp, so I renewed her permit!

One day, a woman came to me whose daughter had just had a baby and the child's father did not have an ID card. The word had spread that I was helping the Palestinian refugees. Some people wanted Iraqi passports because if they were stopped by gangs or even the regular police and provided Palestinian identification, they could be detained, kidnapped, or killed. Many wanted to escape from Iraq. I began to provide them with Iraqi passports for their safety, also because they could not enter any bordering Arab countries with Palestinian travel documents. I became an intermediary between the people and a friend of mine who lived in Ramadi, three hours away from Baghdad. My friend was from a clan that specialized in making passports and documents. I undertook this work despite the dangers of the journey between Baghdad and Ramadi. My task was to take the photographs and information to my friend and return to Baghdad the next day. There were many bandits on the road called *mujahideen* who were from militias, and there were also the Americans. I didn't make any money doing this work, I only asked for enough money to cover transportation. The purpose of my work was humanitarian, not commercial, and my aim was to serve my people, the Palestinians. As a result of this work, many families managed to flee Iraq.

As a result of the chaos of war, Palestinians lost their rights and their Iraqi landlords forced them out of their homes even when they had paid the rent. A camp was set up for them at the Haifa Club, a Palestinian sports club in the Al-Baladiyat area.

A refugee camp set up at Haifa Club

Daily life was so unbearable that several Palestinians tried to leave Iraq completely by going to Jordan. They went to Al Ruwaished, on the border of Iraq and Jordan. A refugee camp had been located there in 1991, for Iraqis fleeing Saddam's regime during the first Gulf War. The camp had long since closed, but in 2003, Palestinians fled to this camp and it was re-opened. My mother was among those who fled. She stayed for only one week. The sandstorms were so fierce and the desert weather was so hot that she felt she couldn't breathe, and she came back to Baghdad. Other Palestinians stayed in that camp, but Jordan would not admit them, so they were stuck on the border. The wait for resettlement abroad was so long that in the end many families came back to Baghdad. Those who bore the harsh desert conditions were finally resettled in Canada, Chile, Brazil, and other countries, after up to four years in the camp.

The hatred of Palestinians intensified among those Iraqis who saw us as being close to Saddam Hussein and his people. This led to arrests, forced displacements, torture and murder. They tortured Palestinians in horrific ways using electricity, drills and acid. Often even if a ransom was agreed upon for a kidnapped Palestinian, the gangs instead returned his mutilated body.

In Baghdad, I tried to get a video camera to document the suffering of our people. I had to rent it from a store in an area called Al-Mashtal. I rented it for fifty dollars for five days and gave a deposit of $300 that I would get back when I returned the camera. I approached Palestinians in many areas in Baghdad including Al-Baladiyat, Al-Hurriya, Topchi, Al-Dora, Saffaranya and Al-Amen. I conducted several interviews with Palestinian families who intended to leave Iraq with the help of my friends, Thamer, Walid, and Abdo. I also rented a car from another friend. It was a very tiring trip and expensive, but I continued for the five days communicating with many of our people. The film was five hours long. Because of my fear of being arrested or killed if I tried to transfer the film to a DVD in Baghdad, I decided to travel outside Iraq in order to do the transfer. I went to a photographer in a Palestinian refugee camp in Damascus. The photographer was able to transfer the film for me. It was a very difficult trip and it cost a lot to travel and to do the transfer.

Illustration of me conducting my interviews

While I was at the refugee camp I talked to many agents at the UNHCR (The United Nations High Commissioner for Refugees) and UNRWA (The United Nations Relief and Works Agency for Palestinians), explaining the threats against Palestinians and how dangerous the situation was for us. They told me that they could not help us while we were in Iraq, but if we were able to leave Iraq and reach the Syrian border, they would be able to help and support us. I returned to Baghdad again. It was an insecure and tense situation there with many people having been arrested and even killed. The targeting of Palestinian families living in the Baghdad compound increased. There were mortar attacks, and more kidnappings. Everything was worse than it was before I left.

*The moment when Americans came searching our neighborhood with their dogs and tanks. Everyone was petrified.*

I began a tour, knocking on the doors of all the Palestinians in Baghdad in order to convince them to get out of Iraq and get to the Syrian border. I had some difficulty convincing some families because of their lack of money and fears that they would repeat the kind of suffering that had happened to our people in Ruwaished Refugee camp on the Jordanian border. Despite that, the majority agreed and planned to leave Iraq because they felt so unprotected and exposed to death at the hands of the militias scattered throughout all the streets in their area.

One day, I was walking on one of the roads and I met a friend of my brother Amer. He was fluent in English, and I noticed that he was walking with two foreigners. They seemed to be American. He introduced them to me. One was named Tom and the other was William. We shook hands and talked a little about the status of the refugees and the persecution and murders that were happening to us. I learned that Tom and William were part of a group called "Christian Peacemaker Teams" who were against all forms of war or violence, and who worked for peace in many countries around the world. I invited them to visit our house and they promised to do that as soon as possible.

The next day they came to my house. The Americans were Tom, Beth, Maxine, and Sheila. There was also a Canadian named Bob. Two interpreters from the Palestinian community were with them. My brother Amer came to meet them and my mother prepared lunch for them. She cooked a Palestinian meal called kofta – meat cooked with tomatoes. After we finished lunch and drank tea together, they thanked my mother and me for the delicious meal. Then we were able to talk some more. We explained that we were Palestinian families that needed help getting out of Iraq to the Syrian border in order to save ourselves from the persecution by the militias.

*Illustration of the kofta my mother made for the Americans.*

I asked them, "How can you help us, and what do you need us to provide for you?"

They said, "We need some information about the refugees so that we can put pressure on the Ministry of the Interior to stop the arrests and prevent the militants from hurting these families."

I replied, "We appreciate your time, but we do not want you to just get information for journalistic purposes. That would be useless. We need to work on a concrete solution. All the families have agreed that their priority is to leave Iraq as soon as possible, since the situation for the Palestinians has become unendurable and continues to get worse."

They asked if there was any other solution. I told them we could not tolerate the situation anymore as it had become too risky. We were determined to leave despite their attempts to convince us that there might be better solutions because of the difficulties that we might face if we tried to leave Iraq with this large number of families. I insisted that we intended to leave Iraq and travel to the Syrian border and that we Palestinian families would travel alone even if they didn't help us. They said that they wanted to help us, and that if that was what we wanted to do they would assist us in every way they could to prevent violence against us, but that their organization did not assist people to emigrate from any country. They explained that Christian Peacemaker Teams (CPT) also did not provide financial assistance, but that they would accompany us in solidarity and do what they could to raise our voices to the world to publicize our plight. Then they said they would go to their headquarters in Al Karrada to discuss the situation and consider how they could be a part of this project. That evening the interpreters called me and said that everyone had agreed to help us by accompanying us to the border. That gave me great strength and lifted my morale.

Photos from when the US bombed Iraq circa 2003

# CHAPTER SIX
# Al-Tanif Camp: 2005

A few days later we had a planning meeting over lunch at the office for Christian Peacemaker Teams. CPT members included Tom, Beth, Bob, Max, Greg, and Sheila, and their interpreter. They lived in a simple apartment in Al Karrada, without security guards or any protection. They were friendly with their neighbors and seemed to have gained the trust of the local people. I noticed that Sheila's smile was nice and friendly. After lunch we discussed how the Palestinian families would be able to cross the Iraqi border. We examined the situation from every possible angle.

The next day, we decided to go to the Green Zone to meet with officials at the UNHCR. We met an Egyptian man who was a very nice and welcoming person. We went with Tom, Sheila and my brother Amer. When we explained the situation to him, he understood the issues and gave us advice and some tips. He agreed that the only solution to end our suffering was to leave Iraq.

Many of the Palestinian families that had decided to leave Iraq left for the Jordanian border, but we wanted to go to the Syrian border despite the harshness of the desert. We saw the desert as more merciful than the danger of brutality by the militias. We needed humanitarian organizations that wanted to help us find solutions and we also needed the coordination of our arrangements with friends who would support us. Initially many of my family and friends were supportive. But as the time came closer, they became afraid. Even though life was so difficult and dangerous for us, the unknown was even more frightening for them. I was dismayed when several of my own cousins decided that they didn't want to continue working with us and even refused to go with us. Despite that, I didn't give up. I decided to go on, to continue this journey and bear all the expenses and any liability myself.

I went to the neighborhood of Al-Salehiya, to the Ghanim transportation company and made a deal with them to transport us to the border. I went back to Al-Baladiyat to consult with the families. We chose October 4, 2005 as the date we would leave Iraq. This was the first day of Ramadan. The families brought their belongings in bags and put them in the garden of our house so we could leave together from my home to travel to the border.

But that same day, I received a call from the Ambassador of Palestine in Iraq. He threatened me that if I did not abandon the plan to travel, he would contact the Iraqi National Guard to arrest and detain the families that intended to leave, including me. I told him that we were not afraid and that threats would not hold us back from our decision. I said that I would leave with them too because we wanted to save our lives and not harm anyone. We had the right to choose our fate.

We were determined to get out and were committed to the deadline. In the evening, the CPT volunteers Tom, Beth, Sheila, Max and their interpreters came to our house. They all agreed to help by accompanying us as nonviolent protection on our trip to the border. I called all the neighbors and friends who were leaving with us to a meeting in order to inform them of the travel plans to reach the Al-Tanif border crossing and try to enter Syria.

While I was consumed with trying to anticipate the unpredictable difficulties that lay ahead, I found myself experiencing warm emotional feelings toward Sheila in my heart. I was impressed with her. I looked at her sitting in front of me, wearing a headscarf out of respect for my culture, and I sensed something strange. I saw a bright future with her. I felt that she would be my wife one day! But I quickly made myself forget about these feelings as I became preoccupied with arranging the trip.

I was also worried about the threat made by the Palestinian ambassador. Some people in the meeting advised me to inform the American forces about the threat made by the ambassador, but I told them that this threat would not affect us. While we were talking, I was surprised to see people arrive who worked for the embassy and who intended to ruin our plan. They made the Palestinian families panic and worry about their safety. I and the CPT volunteers were initially able to calm everyone down and I told them that we were like a train that would continue together on the same track. Nothing would stop us. Just then a person came to the house and told me that there were some people waiting for me in the café close by.

When I went there, I found several prominent Palestinian leaders who were working in organizations loyal to the Palestinian Embassy. They were against Palestinian people leaving Iraq. They were being paid monthly salaries in dollars, which is why I think they were opposing our decision. They tried to convince me to change my decision. I told them that I would leave for the border even if I had to take only one family. Right then I began to think about how to change the travel plans because I was afraid that these people might already know all the details. I told them that ultimately the days ahead would prove to them the sincerity of my words and that leaving Iraq would benefit the families. In the end, they asked if I would be willing to take the responsibility for the families and I told them yes, I would take full responsibility. When I left the coffee shop and returned to the house, I was surprised to find that some of the families had gone back to their homes, and others were taking their bags to go home. I did not know the reason. They had been influenced by the negative voices against us and by their fear of the ambassador, but I knew that these families would continue to be exposed to detention and even death. I decided I would still leave Iraq, even with only one family.

Five families stayed, determined to leave Iraq with me despite the difficulties. All together we were seven men, five women, and seven children. Beth, Tom and Sheila, from the Christian Peacemaker Teams, came with us, along with one interpreter and an Iraqi friend named Sami who was the founder of a group called Muslim Peacemaker Teams.

As we began this journey, you could see the fear on all our faces. As we all boarded a two-decker bus, even while an embassy employee tried to scare us away, we did not know what our fate would be in the desert. But despite the seriousness of the situation and the threats, we had decided to take the risk in order to live in dignity and safety.

At the edge of Baghdad, we ran into an Iraqi checkpoint. A soldier came to the door, and Sheila moved quickly to meet him. She spoke to him in Arabic, showed him her American passport, and said she knew all these people and that everything was in order. He seemed surprised, then waved us through.

All along the way I was thinking of how to find a place to live and provide safety for these families when we arrived. We started to see the sands of the desert as a sign that we were traveling farther away from the city and getting closer to the border. We stopped at a rest area to go to the restrooms. I was worried about the Americans because if the jihadists noticed them, they might be kidnapped. We gave Tom, Beth, and Sheila some Arab clothes and asked them to change. I waited by the door of the bus to check the number to be sure that everyone had come back safely. When I saw Sheila coming back to the bus, I felt my heart pounding.

We continued for about 8 hours, until we arrived at the last Iraqi check point before entering the Syrian border. The Iraqi officer there helped us by stamping our travel documents and giving us permission to leave, even though he knew that the Syrians might not allow us to enter Syria with our Palestinian travel documents.

As we approached the Syrian border, I felt joy mixed with feelings of fear of the unknown. Of course, the border officials would not let us cross, but referred us to the director of the border crossing. I entered his office accompanied by Sheila and Tom. The Syrian official was annoyed and asked why only a few families were leaving Iraq if Palestinians were so threatened and exposed to death. Even though I tried to explain the situation to him it was difficult for him to understand, or perhaps he didn't want to cooperate with us. He threw our documents on

Illustration of the rest stop along the highway to the Syrian border

46

the floor and ordered us to go back to Iraq. He told us that not only would Syria refuse us, but that all other Arab countries would deny us entry because no one accepted these travel documents anymore.

Sheila wept as she spoke to him, standing up for us, and I felt so bad. I tried to reassure her and the others that I still believed everything would be all right. We refused to go back to Iraq, but we were not allowed into Syria, so we just slept on the sidewalk at the border crossing – literally in the middle of the desert, in "no man's land."

Despite the discomfort, this was a beautiful night, because at least we felt safe.

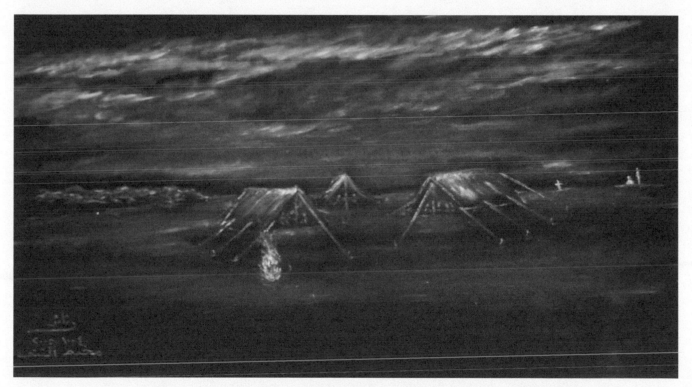

A black velvet oil painting of our camp in no-man's-land near the Syrian border

Women and children sleeping on the sidewalk in the dessert

Some of the original 18 refugees at the makeshift camp near the Syrian border where we
had the best 40 days of our lives

Sheila and children at the refugee camp in Syria where we had the best 40 days of our lives

I woke in the morning with new resolve. Now was the time for us to get to work to help these families. I made a lot of attempts to contact humanitarian organizations, embassies, and the Office of the High Commissioner for Refugees, (the UNHCR). I contacted all those who I knew would draw attention to us.

After three days, the UNHCR responded to me and they visited us. A Danish woman was the leader of the UNHCR group and she was very kind. We told her the whole story: about the threats to the families that made them afraid to leave Baghdad, the people who had been killed or abducted by militias or expelled from their homes, and the danger of militia attacks on the roads going to neighboring countries such as Iran, Kuwait, Saudi Arabia and Turkey. We gave her the names of the people who opposed us including the Palestinian ambassador and told her that we had made many appeals for help to the

Ann Mayman, a UNHCR worker who helped us

UNHCR office. Sheila, Beth and Tom also spoke with her and after listening to everyone she slowly became convinced of our plight. She told us that we were very brave to do what we were doing and that we had the right to UN protection as refugees. She promised to come back the next day and said that she would inform the UNHCR officials about our case. She also said they would send us three tents and that they could treat any small wounds for our group, but they could not provide intensive medical assistance. She added that UNHCR did not want "another Ruwaished Camp," because they would not be able to help a large group of people here.

We were also visited by four men from the Palestinian group Hamas, which was then powerful in Syria. They promised help, but then hung up the phone when we tried to reach them the next day.

On the second day, a group from the UNHCR and UNRWA offices came to assist us with three tents, mattresses, pillows and blankets. The men stabilized the tents with columns and wedges, and we established a camp. Two families shared one tent and each tent was separated by a blanket barrier for privacy. We had lunch and dinner at the cafeteria at the border crossing, and the meals were paid for by UNHCR. We were happy because we felt safe and hopeful. I noticed that everyone was smiling.

Tom Fox, one of the Christian Peacemaker Teams
volunteers who accompanied us.

We spent forty days there and it was one of the best times in my life. I will never forget those forty days. Despite the rough conditions, lack of medical supplies and the harsh weather, we felt free. We felt that we could overcome anything. Make no mistake, the conditions were very challenging. It was very hot during the day and very cold at night. One day a sandstorm hit us that almost blew away the tents. It was so severe that everyone had difficulty breathing. We had to stay in the cafeteria until the end of the storm so that we didn't suffocate and die as we prayed for God to help us.

But slowly we adapted to the situation. Hussein, one of the refugees, was a barber so he cut our hair in the middle of the desert sitting on a rock and holding a mirror in our hand. We taught the children drawing. Despite those difficult days we enjoyed talking and laughing and playing with the children. We ate breakfast and drank tea early in the morning together and then we played soccer and volleyball. At night, we gathered around a fire for warmth. The skies were full of bright stars and we drank coffee and played games like dominos and backgammon and a game called *mahaibes* where a group of people hide a ring in one hand and the other group tries to guess which person has the ring. We sang songs in Arabic and English.

Something else completely unexpected happened to me then. The CPT volunteers stayed with us for the first two weeks, until they felt that we were safe. Sheila, the American CPT volunteer, and I fell in love gradually over those two weeks. Neither of us had planned to ever get married, and we were both surprised by our feelings for each other. I told her I would like to talk with her, and she replied that she would like to talk with me too, but how? When? So we met late at night in the sand dunes, and shared our thoughts and feelings. I even told her that I wanted to marry her, but I did not really want to live in the United States. Since I was currently stuck in the middle of no-man's-land and Sheila was soon to go back to Baghdad and then return to the United States, we had no idea how things would work out. It was also hard to communicate! Sheila spoke only rudimentary Arabic and my English was not very good at all. Later Sheila told her colleague Tom that she loved and admired me, but the problem was the language. We could not fully understand each other. Tom told her that he thought we *did* speak the same language! I think he meant the language of peace and human rights. We spoke about our hopes and dreams. We decided that if we got married, we could be an example of how people of different cultures, backgrounds, and religions could live together in peace.

But our time together was soon to end. The Christian and Muslim Peacemaker Teams volunteers felt that we were now safe, and they had many other projects they needed to return to in Baghdad. Beth and Sami traveled together by car to Baghdad. The interpreter bravely returned by car on his own. It was more dangerous for Sheila and Tom though, because they really did not blend in at all, they were both very fair and Tom was very tall. So they planned to enter Syria and then travel to Baghdad by plane. They requested a 3-day visa to enter the country from the Syrian passport office at the border and after a few days their request was granted. Sheila and I said our farewells. We both had tears in our eyes. It hurt me so much to see her tears. It was like a knife plunged into my heart. Even though she left I felt my soul was still with her, bound to her beauty and goodness.

Life continued in the desert camp. We continued in our routine of cleaning the area, washing clothes, eating, reaching out to embassies of countries who might accept refugees. Ramadan ended, so we even celebrated the Islamic feast of Eid Al-Adha in the middle of the desert. To make the children happy, we made them swings and toys instead of the candy that we would usually give them for the feast. During the Eid, the employees at the cafeteria went on vacation to spend time with their families, so we decided to help the owner by offering to do their work. After work we returned to the camp. We became one family helping one another.

A sketch I drew created from a stain of dirt that was on my shoes

**18** - Sheila's father who came to visit us in 2006

# CHAPTER SEVEN
# Al-Hol Camp: 2005

As the days wore on however, we began to feel fearful that we would be stuck in no-man's-land forever. We were free, but we were not free. We were still waiting for a concrete plan for permanent resettlement. I continued to communicate with the UNHCR and UNWRA and other humanitarian organizations about our situation so that they would put pressure on the Syrian government to allow us to enter the country.

After spending 40 nights in the desert, we received the glorious news that we could enter Syrian territory on humanitarian grounds. We were to stay in a camp located in the Hasakah district in northern Syria. The director of the camp and his assistant visited us. The men with us took down the tents and pulled the pegs and poles from the ground. We could not believe that our suffering had ended after all this time, all the years of fear and anxiety. We entered Syria on November 13, 2005 on buses sent to bring us into the country. We were full of joy and indescribable emotions. For us it was like a victory over the forces of evil and pain. We had safely overcome all the obstacles posed by the checkpoints at the gates of Baghdad, Ramadi, and Fallujah and even the groups of armed fighters.

We called Baghdad to tell the CPT volunteers. When they heard the news, Sheila, Beth, Sami, Omar and Tom were overjoyed for us. We gave thanks to God and embraced each other across the miles in the midst of our joy and happiness. When our families in Iraq heard the good news that we had entered Syria, we began to be overwhelmed with calls from Baghdad. Some of the Palestinian families and young people regretted not having left with us and some families in Baghdad started to knock on my mother's door at all hours of the day and night looking for help in finding a way to join us.

The distance between the Syrian border and Al-Hol camp took nine hours so we stopped at a café to get a bit of rest. We arrived at the camp late at night. There were five mud-built houses which were built in 1991 by Yazidi families who had been living there. We were five families and each family was given a house. We were somewhat afraid as the houses were abandoned and had no lights or electricity, were full of old scrap metal and needed to be cleaned. Because of this the families were forced to stay outside until dawn. Due to the lack of support from the humanitarian organizations, new problems occurred. There was no one to ask for help except the director of the camp who came every week to make a note of what we needed, such as the food (which barely met our needs). We began to become more assertive and increased our requests for electricity, water, food and medicine. Not to be completely dependent on them, we also decided to work outside the camp for daily subsistence. However, we did not have the approval of the camp director for this. The Syrian security agencies started to visit us in order to get information about each of us, and this pressure caused us a lot of stress. After this we were provided with food rations, bedding and a tank of water each week for drinking and washing. We began to take walks to get to know the people living in the surrounding area. We did not have any money to buy mobile phone cards, so we were forced to sell things from our supplies of food and bedding in order to contact the humanitarian organizations, the commission or our families. When we managed to get phone cards Sheila and I spoke together, and she promised to come and visit us on her way home to the United States. Two months after we entered the camp, she came. We were ecstatic! She planned to stay with us for two weeks and she promised to help us. She had recently heard from a Canadian woman who had offered to sponsor us to emigrate as refugees to Canada.

However, the peace of those weeks with Sheila was shattered. While Sheila and I were on a walk together, Sheila received a call from her CPT colleague Greg in Baghdad, informing her that an armed group had kidnapped Tom and three other members of CPT. This was a great shock to all of us, as we had all known Tom. The children were inconsolable, the adults were extremely upset that a militia would kidnap a humanitarian activist. I offered to return to Baghdad to help CPT, but Sheila refused, as she knew my life would be in danger there. She, however, cut her visit short and traveled to Jordan, where CPT had asked her to go to help with the crisis response. The kidnapping apparently was big news, and the team needed people in Jordan to help with media response and coordinating in case of release of the captives.

Entrance to Al-Hol Camp

All of us relaxing in the desert at night

A studio I made to display my art

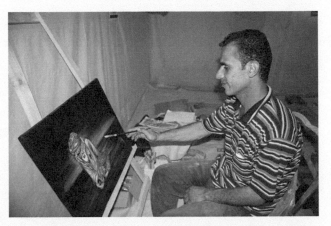

Me in the art studio I put together in Al-Hol Camp

Some of the art I posted in the art gallery
in Al-Hol Camp

A photo of all the refugees and Sheila at Al-Hol Camp in 2006

So we were left to continue on our own. Problems between the families began to arise because of the pressures of unemployment, a lack of facilities, harassment from the Syrian security agencies and endless, endless waiting. We felt as if we were walking through a dark tunnel desperately searching for scraps of hope and some certainty about our future. This caused me a lot of mental distress and it got to the point where I was suffering episodes of fainting and oral paralysis. As a result, I was sent to a clinic and treated with injections, nutrients and painkillers. When I recovered, I decided to open a studio or workshop where I could draw and paint again and in doing so express my internal pain and anxieties through works of art. As I did not possess any paints or even a chair to sit on, I had to travel outside of the area to Hasakah to get decent materials. The city was one hour away from the camp, so I had to get permission from the camp administration to go. A friend and I set out together. The sun was shining when we began our journey but later it began to rain, and the ground turned into mud that quickly buried our feet. We decided to go to a café and as I was sitting there, I noticed my mud-encrusted shoe – the mud had created a picture resembling the figures of a man and a woman. It made me think of Sheila and wonder if we would ever be together again.

When we went back to the camp without bringing any decent art materials from the city I was forced to paint on pieces of cheap black velvet. I still have some of those paintings. I poured my worries and problems into my drawings and paintings and created a simple exhibition in the camp that we constructed by putting up white fabric on the walls of the tent. With the help of one of the refugees who was an electrician, we hung up lamps. However, the site of the exhibition was not very safe because of the nature of the desert environment. In the summer, snakes and scorpions came in from the desert and in the winter, insects came seeking warmth. Even so, the exhibition was visited by a Tunisian official from the UNHCR with two ladies who worked for the American Department of Foreign Affairs. I gave them one of my paintings as an expression of gratitude for their visit.

We decided to find ways to alleviate the suffering of the refugee families caused by the stress and boredom. The first people to initiate this were Abu Ali who opened a barbershop in the middle of the camp, and Abu Omar who had permission to work in a car repair shop outside the camp. After first prohibiting it, the administration gradually allowed us to go down into the villages surrounding the Al-Hol camp to mix with the local Syrian people and get to know them. We formed friendships with the local Syrian families and were often invited to eat with them in their homes. We met some very good-hearted people including two of the camp guards, two of the drivers, and many others not mentioned here. We had some very good times together.

One day in early March 2006, I took one of the children to the barbershop. While he was getting his hair cut, we heard a radio news report that the armed group had both kidnapped and then killed Tom Fox, the

CPT volunteer who had helped us. The child I was with broke into tears, as Tom had been like a father to the children during our weeks in the desert. He had made them laugh, played with them and cared for them to ease some of the pain of exile and deprivation. Many humanitarian and human rights organizations had made many calls for the release of the four abductees. After 100 days in captivity only three were rescued by American and British forces – Jim Loney, Harmeet Sooden and Norman Kember, as you can read in news reports of that time. But Tom Fox had been sold to another militia weeks before. On March 10, 2006, his body, which bore gunshot wounds, was found dumped on the roadside. Tom did not deserve to be killed. He was an American who took a humanitarian stance towards everyone. The fact that he was American did not give anyone the right to murder him. He was not a soldier but a humanitarian and human rights activist.

Despite our grief and sadness, we continued to try to find a permanent solution to our troubles. Sheila continued to help us through her contact in Canada who sent us application forms for refugee status. A human rights volunteer from Sweden who spoke standard Arabic came to stay with us for a week and helped us to fill out the forms and send them to the Canadian Embassy. We had some wonderful times with him. Sheila and I remained in touch with one another long distance. I walked the length and breadth of the camp feeling together with her as I talked to her about our situation and the work we had to do. She promised to visit us for a second time and this time we talked about ways to help the families who had stayed in Baghdad.

Huge efforts were being made to help those Palestinians still stuck in Baghdad. Part of the plan was for the families to come to Syria, but the plan was changed because of the influence of a member of Hamas within Iraq. Instead the families headed for Jordan, but they were not permitted to enter the country and stayed at the border for three months. After cooperation with the Hamas movement in Syria, an agreement was made with the Syrian government for them to enter Al-Hol camp. This was a political rather than a humanitarian decision. In contrast, when our group of five families entered the camp it was based on humanitarian grounds. When the new families arrived, we helped the UNHCR workers set up around 250 tents over two days. It was a joy to welcome the newly arrived families to the camp. These were members of our families, friends and companions and when they arrived, we felt as though we were in our hometowns again.

Later, people from Hamas pressured me to become a member of their group. But I refused to join or to support them. They had not helped us when we were in the Al-Tanif camp for 40 nights. They also sent a representative to try to convince us not to go to Canada. They didn't like it when Muslims emigrated to western countries. The representative offered us furnished accommodations in the Yarmouk camp for Palestinian refugees near Damascus. He also promised to help our young people get married and find work. All of this to make us give up on the idea of traveling to a safer country! To convince the Hamas representative that we meant what we said, I gathered all the families together so that he could hear the refusal directly from them. They did not want his help. They wanted to emigrate to a safer country. Hamas then began to work against me by recruiting people to cause me harm. They harassed me personally and, through the strong relationship between Hamas and the Syrian regime, used their influence against me.

More and more Palestinian families were fleeing Baghdad. Eventually I learned through a friend in the Iraqi border security that the Syrian government was now refusing the Palestinian refugees fleeing from Baghdad, so the Iraqi government was not letting them out across the border. This decision led to the opening of two camps, one on each side of the border: Al-Waleed Camp in Iraq, and Al-Tanif Camp in Syria. Al-Tanif camp was filled by more than 1000 people, when the Iraqi government stopped letting the Palestinians out. So the Al-Waleed camp was formed, just inside the Iraqi border.

The Waleed, Al-Tanif, and Al-Hol camps worked together and were in constant communication. I began to work with members of each camp to organize and extend support for the families fleeing from Baghdad. The new families in the camp asked me to bring them the application forms for emigrating to Canada. I sent faxes to the European embassies in Damascus in order to help them. Some European organizations tried to come to the camps, but the Syrian intelligence agencies prevented them. This was due to the influence of the same Hamas member, who was a Palestinian born in Iraq and who had gangs under his control. They were in charge of the Palestinians both in the camps and in Damascus, and they were working with the Syrian government. He continued to argue that we should not help families to emigrate and that they would help us with food and clothing and even an apartment, but I refused. This made Hamas very angry with me.

In 2006, Sheila and her father came to Al Hol camp to stay with us for one week. They traveled nine hours from Damascus to Hasakah and an hour from Hasakah to the camp. They brought new high-quality art materials for me, and gifts for the children. At the time, her father was in poor health due to a small cancerous growth on his kidney. He was due to have surgery in America, but he postponed the operation to come with Sheila to meet us refugees! We were invited to the mud hut of one of the original refugee families to eat pastries and drink soda. On one laughter-filled visit we were all sitting together, and one of the refugees began to read Sheila's father's palm using cigarette ash. He said, "There is a number in your life which will be close to you." It later turned out that this number was the number of the flight on which her father returned to America! We took a lot of photographs of those happy times during that visit. One night, the men shared a hookah (a water pipe) under the stars with some beer and much laughter. Sheila had told her father that we were in love and wanted to get married. He told us he was very happy about this and had no objections. I thanked him and he repeated how happy he was and invited me to have a beer with him soon in Boston, Massachusetts where he lived. Sheila, her father, and I went to Damascus where Sheila entered the Canadian embassy to lobby on behalf of the families.

# CHAPTER EIGHT

# 70 Days in Prison: 2007

After Sheila and her father returned to the United States, Sheila applied to the American Embassy in the United States for a fiancé visa for me. However, the USCIS (United States Citizenship and Immigration Services) sent the application to Jordan instead of Syria. To correct the mistake, I had to go to the American embassy in Damascus, even though that was dangerous for me. Because of my relationship with Sheila, an American, the Syrian government thought I was connected to the CIA or otherwise a threat to them. In addition, I had attracted attention by sending faxes to multiple foreign embassies, asking for permanent refuge for all the Palestinians who had fled Iraq. I traveled frequently to and from Damascus working on this project. Some of my friends warned me about these activities, and I knew that Hamas didn't like it that I was trying to get refuge in Western countries, but I did not stop.

One day, while I was resting in the Al Hol camp, I saw a security officer riding a motorcycle. He came to my hut and told me that I had to sign a paper and present myself to the General Security Department in the Qamishli Governorate which was three hours away. I thanked him and he left, but I did not make the trip because I had no money for travel that day. The security officer came back the next day and gave me a card saying I would be arrested if I did not go to the Security Department. So the next day I went to the bus station and bought a ticket and rode through the desert for three hours to al-Qamishli to find out why they had called me. The security building had pale concrete walls covered with black soot. I knew that this place was a prison as well as an office, and I knew that behind those black-soot walls were countless stories of innocent people who had died from torture. I waited for a few minutes in the entrance hall on the ground floor, and I felt frightened and cold. Then an officer came to lead me to the director. When I entered his office, his face seemed angry and he asked why I did not come to the office when summoned earlier that week. I explained that I lived in the Al Hol refugee camp and that it was difficult to earn money for travel.

"Hah," he said, "but you can go to the embassies to ask for help!" I tried to stay calm and answered that I did not go to any embassy. "You have to go sign another paper at the Intelligence Department," he waved his finger at me and dismissed me. I was escorted back to the station. The main Intelligence Department was nine hours away by bus, at my own expense. I was on the bus all night. When I arrived in the morning I was in a state of stress and anxiety, with a whirlpool of questions endlessly circling through my mind. An officer was waiting for me and took me in a taxi to the main building where I waited with my heart in my throat.

I never did go back to the Al Hol camp. From the Intelligence Department I was sent to Far' Filistin, a political prison. I was imprisoned there for 70 days, first all alone in a cell where my shoes served as a pillow, then in an underground room where forty prisoners were crammed together like sardines. The door was black, with small windows up high, and yellow lights on top. The blankets were dirty and infested with bugs. I was interrogated by two officers, one seeming to be friendly, the other being very mean. I was blindfolded and tortured, with beatings on my legs while my feet were immobilized in a truck tire, and with ice cold showers with my hands tied behind my back. I was moved from place to place. Praying or reading the Koran was forbidden. We were starving, being fed one boiled egg for breakfast, and sharing one chicken among 40 people for dinner. Worst of all was hearing the screams and cries for help of other prisoners being tortured, including women and children. It was frightening to hear the sound of the guards' footsteps and keys turning in heavy door locks. It was horrible and I began to lose hope. An immigration judge ordered me moved to another prison. There my mother visited me with my brother Amer, and they brought me clothes and food. When Sheila learned of my detention, she was furious. She got in contact with Amnesty International and other humanitarian organizations on my behalf and sent a letter to the Syrian president Bashar Al-Assad, but nothing helped. She told me later that she barely slept the whole time I was in prison.

I blame all of my suffering on the Hamas member who worked as a double-agent in Syria, taking money meant for the refugees and pocketing it himself, also reporting on Palestinian refugees like me and causing us untold suffering.

Instead of being set free, I was deported to the Iraqi border. This was a mean and worthless action with no basis in law. An international ruling and agreement with the Red Cross states that no person who is seeking asylum can be forcibly returned to the country he or she has come from. However, the authorities justified my situation by saying that I had entered Syria illegally. In this way, this Hamas member conspired against me. I would have liked to tell him, who was one of our own people, that in our worst times he abandoned us, and he put many families in prison. Some of these families I know by name. He did nothing to help us but rather he hurt us and worked with the Syrian government against us to destroy our efforts to emigrate to Canada. Now I want to tell everyone not to ever be afraid. Speak up for honesty and truth and solidarity against oppression, lies and injustice. If everyone did this, the world would change for the better.

When I was taken from Syria to the border, the UNHCR asked the Al-Tanif camp officials if I could stay there for just one night so that someone from the Canadian embassy could come and meet with me. The next day a Canadian Embassy employee came with an American human rights supporter of the Palestinians in Iraq. They tried to cross the border to meet me but ended up stuck there for three hours because the Syrian authorities would not allow them to enter to meet me without an agreement with the Syrian Interior Ministry. In the end, I did not have the good fortune to meet the Canadian delegation. Now the border administration was forced to hand me over to the Iraqi side. However, I refused to surrender to this. I begged an Iraqi policeman not to take me into Iraq as I had an appointment with the Canadian officials. The policeman told me to go with him to the border to finish some procedures and that he would then release me. I agreed only if he would help me get on a bus entering Syria. He agreed when I offered him $100 and told a bus driver to drop me off in the refugee camp on the Syrian side of the border.

So, I was able to escape getting deported, and instead I stayed on the Syrian side of the border, in the Al-Tanif camp. For one month, I stayed alone in a small tent, weary and hidden from sight. Nobody knew I was there except for a few close friends. During this time, I was in constant contact with the UNHCR, waiting for them to get permission to come and see me. I was also in touch with Sheila. I faced a lot of trials during my stay in that tent. On one occasion a friend called inviting me to eat with him in a tent some distance from mine. Going back to my tent, I felt as though someone was surreptitiously observing me, and while I was watching TV via satellite, I was filled with the feeling that someone was circling the tent. The satellite signal started to break up which indicated someone was passing by the dish. I was filled with fear and the sense that something was about to happen. A man in military uniform entered. He was Syrian. He looked astonished to see me in this worn-out tent far away from anywhere. He told me to go with him. I put on my shoes and clothes quickly. A whole group of Syrian soldiers had surrounded the tent and a military jeep had pulled up on the main road next to it. I was led to the vehicle and put inside. They took me to the Syrian border officer. He was pale-faced and completely devoid of humanity. He slapped me hard in the face and detained me all day in a dark, dank room filled with an unbearable smell of filth. There was no mattress and I spent a very cold, hard night lying on the ground.

The next day I was taken to Tadmor Prison which was four hours away from Al-Tanif. I was imprisoned there for four days and questioned about why I entered Syria without permission. I explained the reasons I had crossed the border, telling them that if I had entered Iraq, I would have been murdered by Shia militias. I also told them that someone from the Canadian embassy should be coming to meet me and I was waiting for them. They wanted me to sign what I had told them, then they rewrote the report and I signed it. It was then decided that I should be sent to the Al-Tanif camp and I was so relieved. Unfortunately, this did not happen. Instead they sent me back to the vast and terrifying Far' Filistin political prison ("Palestinian Branch Prison") in Damascus, and I began to lose hope. I was brought to see an officer who said, "You again. Why are you back here? Weren't you set free? What happened to you?"

I told him, "I can't go back to Iraq because the militias are targeting Palestinians. If I go back it will mean certain death for me. Also, I am waiting to meet with officials from the Canadian Embassy."

I then asked the officer to place me in Al-Hol camp under house arrest until my meeting with the Canadian Embassy staff. He dismissed what I told him, but I stayed in Far' Filistin for 20 days, honestly I lost track. This prison is considered one of the worst in Syria. Detainees here are tortured in the most brutal ways.

Disease is rampant and there is very little health care or decent food. They practiced solitary confinement. While there I was told that there was a prisoner who had been in solitary for one and a half *years*. They put me in a solitary cell which had filthy black walls, a rusty door and harsh lights that hurt my eyes. There were insects everywhere. I couldn't sleep at night because of my anxiety and constant thoughts and the cries of nearby women and children.

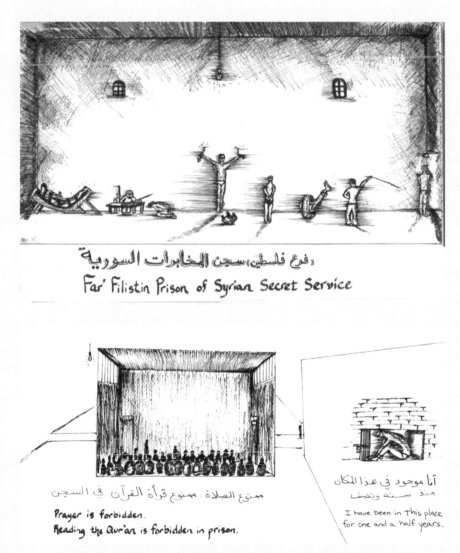

فرع فلسطين، سجن المخابرات السورية
Far' Filistin Prison of Syrian Secret Service

ممنوع الصلاة. ممنوع قراءة القرآن في السجن.
Prayer is forbidden.
Reading the Qur'an is forbidden in prison.

أنا موجود في هذا المكان
منذ سنة ونصف
I have been in this place
for one and a half years.

Sketches of the prison in Syria where I was imprisoned for 70 days

67

Another Palestinian from Iraq from the Al-Hurriyah district of Baghdad had been arrested and accused of crossing through Lebanon to enter Syria illegally. He was very quiet and knew how to draw. A decision was made to send him to Iraq. A few days later, my papers were sent to the judge who ruled that I too should be returned to Iraq. I asked her if I could speak but she refused to listen to me. She said it was not her decision and I was deported to Iraq a second time. When we got to the border, I was handed over to the American forces who were supervising the border at that time. I was put in a border prison for four days because I did not have identity papers or travel documents with me. These were in the Al-Hol camp with the director who deliberately delayed sending them to me. After four days, the officer told me that they were going to send me to the Iraqi Interior Ministry. I was terrified. I was afraid I was going to die from torture at their hands. I quickly called Sheila on my mobile and said, "Sheila, they are going to send me to the Interior Ministry." She began to cry. She knew what would happen if I was handed over to them. I felt like I was already dying and wanted to say some final words. "Sheila, all I want you to do is to continue your studies, get good grades, and fulfill your ambition to be a doctor...I will see you again." Sheila could barely speak in reply. I looked out of the prison window at the birds in the sky. The air was fresh. I then said to her, "I feel safe now."

But just in time, that day my documents arrived from the Al Hol camp, and I was able to identify myself to the Americans. When I gave my documents to the Americans, they treated me well and decided I did not have to be sent back into Iraq. I felt oddly reassured and safe with them. One of the Iraqi officers even cut my hair and brushed the cuttings off my face with a towel the way barbers do. Some American soldiers, accompanied by an interpreter, came to pick me up. I told them that my fiancée was an American. The soldier asked me my name and when I said "Thaer" he surprised me by saying that lots of people were fighting to get me out. I was known by a lot of people. This was all thanks to Sheila who had contacted several friends, humanitarian organizations and charities as well as the UNHCR.

While in the border prison, I was visited by a fellow refugee and human rights activist named Qusay. I had previously spoken to him by mobile phone about how he could enter the camp. He visited me several times and tried to help me get out of prison. He was a very kind and good-hearted person. Some days later an official from UNHCR contacted me after Sheila wrote to him. He asked me if any of the Iraqi officers had attacked me. I told him no, that I had not been attacked. He then told me that he was coming to get me that day, and he did. He came and got me out of prison in February of 2007. After my release, Qusay and I walked for half an hour in the direction of Al-Waleed camp. When we arrived, I was surprised to see another Palestinian there who had been in the Far' Filistin prison with me.

# CHAPTER NINE
# Al-Waleed Camp and My Return to Baghdad 2007

I arrived at Al-Waleed and they brought me inside the camp. It had been decided that I would live with two other young men. Life inside the camp began. As a result of my imprisonment and torture in Syria and the lack of food and sleep, my face bore clear signs of struggle, exhaustion and mental distress. I decided to use my time in the camp to rest and recuperate. The exhaustion soon overwhelmed me. While eating lunch that first day, I was overcome by lethargy. I did not even have the strength to go wash my hands after lunch, but fell asleep where I lay in my tent.

After a few days, I gradually began to get better and decided to take a walk around by myself. I called Sheila and told her about the poor state of my health. She set out to help me once again, this time attempting to get me to Jordan. She called an employee named Michelle in the UNHCR in Amman and asked for a meeting. We did indeed meet at Al-Waleed and this led to rapid efforts being made to get me a visa to enter Jordan. The plan was that I would go to the American embassy in Amman to apply for a visa to the US based on my engagement to Sheila. Unfortunately, the Jordanian authorities prevented me from entering their territory as I was carrying a Palestinian travel document that had been issued in Iraq. Then a Red Cross employee came to ask why I had been put in prison. He was also shocked that I had been removed from Syria to Iraq. He referred to the international law which prohibits a country from sending a refugee back to the country that he or she has fled due to persecution and threat to their life. In addition to this,

Amnesty International contacted me from their British office to find out about the human rights violations I had experienced. An Algerian man along with many other people took my information and tried to help. However, all this was to no avail.

On one of my walks through the camp, I saw my Aunt Zakiya with her son Mahmoud. They had a tent at the far end of the camp where the numbers had swelled as more and more families fled from death in Baghdad. After this chance meeting, I began to spend most of my time in my Aunt Zakiya's tent. She and her daughter-in-law made all kinds of food for me for breakfast, lunch and dinner including hot sandwiches filled with cheese, olive oil and *Zataar*, a mixture of herbs. She was a very kind and goodhearted person who welcomed and took care of me.

Later the camp was hit by a powerful dust storm that blew into our midst. Some tents were even ripped up from the ground. My tentmates and others went to shelter in a safe place, but I decided to stay in the tent. I had a tape player and listened to loud music so that I didn't feel afraid. Many refugees suffered severe respiratory illnesses because of this storm. Some had been suffering from asthma that was exacerbated by the constantly changing climate and frequent storms, as well as a lack of food and medical supplies.

During my time in the camp I took early morning walks towards the hills where I stopped to contemplate the safety and freedom I had gained since I was released from prison. I breathed in the early morning air as the rays of the sun began to illuminate the camp in the middle of the beautiful desert which stretched as far as the eye could see. I felt more energy and decided to get back to work. My friend Wael and I decided to offer something to the children in the camp by teaching them art. We got a tent for a classroom from Qusay who was responsible for the camp. Many families told us that they wanted to enroll their children in our free classes, but we did not have any materials for drawing. I told Sheila what we needed to teach the children and she called Michelle from UNHCR in Amman and asked her to visit the camp and bring us what we needed from Jordan. This was done at Sheila's personal expense that she considered a donation from her to the children of Al-Waleed. Michelle brought the materials and we began to give the children daily lessons. Then we encountered the problem of temperature. It was extremely hot inside the tent as there was no way to cool or ventilate it. Despite this and the suffering and daily worries of life in the camp, the children were constantly smiling, and their hearts were full of joy. They expressed both their joy and their pain through drawing which acted as a healing remedy for their minds and spirits.

At Al-Waleed refugee camp where I taught the kids how to paint during the summer. Our painting studio was just a tent to shelter us from the hot summer sun.

Despite this meaningful work, I felt oppressed by the ongoing anxiety and boredom of camp life. When hundreds of people are packed together in such conditions, interpersonal problems flare and relationships fray. After some time living in the camp, I decided to take a tent set apart from the rest of the refugees in order to avoid being drawn into the many interpersonal problems of the young people living there. I got to know someone else who also wanted to live apart from the main camp. His name was Bisam and he was quite good at English. We became good friends and began to share our problems.

Finally, I decided to return to Baghdad. It was futile waiting in the camp. I decided to risk traveling back into Iraq to get an Iraqi passport. My plan was to use it to travel to Turkey via Baghdad International Airport. There were families in the camp who, with the help of the UNHCR, were traveling to Baghdad to get medical treatment. I took the opportunity to go with them and booked two seats on the bus for my aunt and me. We began our journey and traveled as far as the Ramadi district, where the driver stopped the bus in an agricultural area and told us we would have to spend the night here. A rule had been brought in by the American forces prohibiting the movement of vehicles after 6 pm and any car found breaking this rule would be shot at. I will never forget that terrible night next to a farm. We could not sleep because of the large mosquitoes devouring us. At dawn the air freshened, and the bus set off again. We arrived in Baghdad and then headed toward the Baladiyat district.

Before the bus reached Baladiyat I asked the driver to drop me off on my own. I was scared for my life and did not want to attract anyone's attention or for anyone to know that I had arrived. I had heard that the Iraqi government was searching for me and asking the people in the area about my whereabouts. I wore a hat and glasses and went to the home of my older sister, Siham. Her flat was on the third floor. When she heard my knock, she looked through the peephole in the door and recognized me right away, despite my disguise. She opened the door and she and her children threw their arms around me. They were so happy to see me. I called Sheila and told her that I had arrived, and she wept tears of joy and relief. She had been extremely worried about me. I told her about my plan to get an Iraqi passport and use it to travel to Turkey.

I stayed a week in my sister's flat without going outside. When I could no longer stand it, I went out into the neighborhood and began to make cautious enquiries about who could make the passport. I found out about a person called Ahmed and went to see him. He requested a sum of money which I gave him and then he told me it would take a week. During this second week of waiting, I slept in our old flat where my younger brother Tarik was living. My mother was in Syria. I suggested that we sell the flat and go to Turkey together and from there to any country we could settle in. He refused. I tried to convince him not to stay in the flat in Baghdad, but he insisted. I decided to travel alone. However, Ahmed had encountered some difficulties and was taking a long time to make the passport. I couldn't help but reflect on how I had been the one to provide passports for everyone, but now I couldn't get one for myself. I gave Ahmed another chance despite the danger in the area.

Every day houses were being searched by American and Iraqi forces. I kept moving from place to place and slept on the roofs of different homes every night, sometimes my sister's and sometimes the homes of my friends Rafat and Waleed. There were long power outages and the heat was intense. All the time I was waiting for my passport, but it didn't come. I took my money back from Ahmed and was forced to look for someone else. I found someone who promised to get it for me in one week. I gave him the money and told him I wanted an official passport as I was going to leave from the airport. At that time the new G series passports were being issued that had different covers. He agreed to make me one like this and I got my passport.

I went to a travel agent in Bab Al-Sharji Al-Sadoun in the city center to get my ticket to Turkey and I also made a temporary hotel reservation which would allow me to get a visa at the airport. I started to prepare to leave. I was very apprehensive, but there was no other choice for me.

My niece's husband Zaki was working as a driver and I arranged for him to take me to the airport the next day. I tried to give him the fare, but he refused to take it despite my insistence. I got out of the car and said goodbye to him and joined the queue of people waiting to go one by one through security and past the police dogs. After I got through this stage, I reached the area where we dropped off our baggage. It was then time for the passport to be inspected. I waited in line as one by one the travelers went up to the window to see the officer who stamped the passports. I didn't wait long. The person in front of me was called forward and I knew it would be my turn next. As I stood there the fear started to gradually creep up from my stomach and into my head. I felt as though I was stuck to the ground. I had to use all my strength to force myself to quickly walk forward. I stopped in front of the officer and said, "Salaam Alaykum" in an Iraqi accent, hoping to win him over. He returned my greeting and I gave him my passport. He turned to the computer, which was in the corner of his small, cabin-like room and began to type in some details. He opened the passport and entered it into the machine. The machine beeped and without looking at me the officer took the passport and examined it. I cannot describe that moment. It was terrifying. I didn't know what my fate was going to be. He turned and looked at me, then picked up the stamp, stamped the passport and handed it back to me, and I went to the departure lounge. It was a big room. I was afraid I would see an Iraqi who lived in our area who would recognize me and inform the Iraqi authorities. The time for departure was announced and one by one we began to enter the gate which led to the plane. I took my seat and the flight attendants began the safety instructions. I think the plane had Russian markings. The plane took off. It ascended in a spiral movement to avoid being hit by fighter rockets. When it got up into the sky it began to fly naturally, and I took a deep breath. I felt a sense of freedom but then I remembered this was not really freedom as I still had no secure home or citizenship in the world.

# CHAPTER TEN

# Istanbul and the Nightmare Journey to Greece

I arrived at Istanbul airport in July 2007. As we entered Turkish airspace I looked out of the window at the distant roads, farms and the beautiful green country. I was so happy to see this sight. The captain told us to fasten our seatbelts to prepare for landing. After we had landed safely the passengers burst into warm applause for the pilot and the flight attendants for getting us to Turkey safely. We got off the plane and headed toward the arrival lounge where the routine inspections took place. I was feeling clear signs of exhaustion from the journey. I couldn't believe I was still able to walk upright. Thank God for everything, and Sheila. I went to the baggage claim, got my suitcase and headed out of the airport.

I was wondering how to talk and act in this country, about which I knew next to nothing. I didn't know the language or anything about the lives of the people who lived there. As I went out the main airport door, I heard some people speaking Arabic. I stopped and listened, wondering if they could possibly be Iraqi. I then greeted them and asked their help in finding the address of the hotel. One of them replied, "I am staying in that hotel! I can show you the way." We took a taxi to the hotel and I stayed there for a few days. My plan was to find a way to Greece, where I could apply for refugee status. I needed to find a human smuggler to help me get there. I met some people who were staying at the hotel who also hoped to get to Greece. My brother Thamer had given me the number of a smuggler. I spoke with this man on the phone and I agreed to pay him $1,500 to get me to Greece. We met and I gave him the money. He promised me I would be in Greece in a week's time, so I had to stay longer in the hotel in Istanbul.

In order to get to know the place I wandered through the alleys, markets and neighborhoods looking at the buildings and shops. The things I liked the best were the beautiful blue Mediterranean, the seagulls and the fresh clean air. One day as I was walking along one of the streets, I saw someone whose face looked familiar. I thought I may have seen him in Al-Baladiyat in Baghdad. Seeing him made me miss my family and friends even more. I approached him. "Do you live in Baladiyat?"

"Yes, I live there" he replied. I shook hands with him and introduced myself. His name was Muthana. We got to know each other and began to sit and talk together until we became friends. It turned out that he too intended to flee to Greece via the same smuggler, who arranged for people to be smuggled into Greece via rubber dinghies. We took the seven-hour bus ride from Istanbul to Izmir and were met at the garage by a man from Gaza City who worked with our smuggler. We decided to stay the night in a small hotel room until it was time to continue the journey.

Three days later we were told to go to the garage and take a bus with 25 Iraqis to the town of Marmaris and from there we would travel to Greece. Marmaris was a tourist destination, magically beautiful with stunning views of the ocean. Almost all the other refugees intended to go to Greece via the same smuggler. They had fled wars and persecution in their countries and had spent all their money on this venture. When we arrived in Marmaris, with its peace, greenery and beauty, we were told that we had to stay in one of the hotels. To be honest, I started to think it had all been a mistake. I was not reassured by all this moving about from place to place. In the end, we stayed in a hotel for one night. At daybreak they told us we had to stand at a certain point next to the sea because a big boat was coming to take us to Greece. We followed their instructions and stood in the designated spot, waiting and waiting. We walked up and down looking at the restaurants, the landmarks and the tourists. When midnight came, nothing had happened. The smuggler had changed the plan on the pretext that the weather was unsuitable for going out to sea. Weary and frustrated, I phoned him in a state of fury. Screaming at him over the mobile phone, I told him that what he was doing was not right and I wanted my money back. I was ready to go back to Istanbul to get my money from him, but the smuggler managed to calm me down and promised me that everything would be OK. We would only have to wait one more night and he would find another way to transport us. He said there were several different ways to get to Greece both by sea and through the forests, but the sea route was the best and the least expensive.

We didn't stay in a hotel that night because we did not have enough money left for an expensive tourist hotel. Instead we spent the night on benches next to the sea with nothing to cover us. We were shaking with cold and completely exhausted from hunger and lack of sleep. At dawn, the smuggler told us we had to go to an area called *Fatiha*, in Arabic, that was four hours from Marmaris. We got the bus tickets from a travel agent. There were a lot of passengers, mostly Iraqis. We set off. During the journey, we were stopped at a Turkish security checkpoint to be searched. We got off the bus one by one and they began to frantically search our bags, demanding that we get out our passports and papers, which they took. They then told us to follow them to a military office. They said they wanted to question us about the large number of people on the bus, claiming that this had aroused their suspicions since we were going to a tourist area. In the end, they decided to arrest us.

They kept us in prison for two days. The nights there were terrible. We were suffering from hunger, cold and lack of sleep as we could not find any good place to rest. In the early morning, we were questioned by an officer who spoke fluent standard Arabic. Two people whose Turkish visas had expired were told they would be deported back to Iraq. But then they let the rest of us go, because we had visas that were current and not expired.

I began to feel suspicious, wondering if all these obstacles and problems were mere coincidence or if the smuggler was behind them. I called him again and demanded my money back. Muthana and I started the nine-hour return trip to Istanbul and once we arrived there were able to get our money back from the smuggler. We returned to Izmir and found a hotel. Once again, we started to look for another way to escape. A lot of smugglers frequented this hotel as well as the local cafes and restaurants. We met a Sudanese man who took money from us saying he could get us to Greece in a week's time. We waited a week and then another week but to no avail, so we took our money back again. We found another smuggler who was an Iraqi. He was a short, bespectacled man with US residency. He named a price; we gave him the money and he promised that he would transport us in a week. He kept his promise and soon called us, telling us to be ready that evening. He instructed us to bring clothes to change into when we reached the island and to put them in a tightly sealed bag so they wouldn't get wet. Muthana and I bought life jackets.

A man came to the hotel and told us to follow him. After a five-minute walk from the hotel, we reached a Jeep waiting for us that could hold about ten people. We were very relieved. Then more people began to arrive intending to take the same journey. At one point, there were 25 of us, including a family with three small children. The windows were darkened, and I felt the lack of air as the space was very cramped and we were packed in like sardines. It was hard to breathe, and I began to feel angry and frustrated during the three-and-a-half-hour drive to the sea near the Izmir airport. The driver started to give us instructions via an interpreter who spoke Arabic and Turkish. He told us to put on our life jackets and that when he stopped the car next to the sea, we should quickly jump out of the car and head for the boat. This had to be done in less than a minute, so the police did not see us. It was so hot and cramped that I could not put on my life jacket. Others tried to put them on as they ran to the water because the boat was waiting for us in the water some distance from the beach. It was small. We ran towards it, jumping into the water. Our clothes were instantly soaking wet. When we reached the boat, we grabbed at the sides, but it was difficult to climb into it. We helped the little children and their family into the boat then everyone made sure they had their life jackets on. As the sun went down, the Turkish captain started the engine and we headed toward the Island of Mytilene.

*An oil painting I did of our journey to Mytilene Island in 2007*

To go there legally in a straight line from the place where we had set off would have taken half an hour. To get there illegally took three hours. When we were halfway there, the motor died. There we were, in the middle of the huge seemingly endless sea and the water began to rise and enter the boat. The water was coming in so fast that the boat started to tilt. There were so many of us, much more than the boat should have been carrying. Terrified that we would drown, all of us -- men, women and children -- started to bail out the water until the boat regained its balance. The captain was able to start the engine again and we continued on the way.

We were packed into the boat so tightly that Muthana sat on my knees for three hours which was agonizing. However, this was a bittersweet pain and I endured it for the sake of my friend. The sight of him made me feel as if I was with my family. As the boat moved forward and the sound of the waves rang in my ears, I looked at the sky and the stars and it gave me a sense of peace and comfort. I told myself, "At last you will see Sheila. You will meet her again and your eyes will be filled with the sight of her and you will hold her to your chest like a child." When I heard the calls of the white seagulls I felt as though they were whispering to me, "Don't worry, you will soon be with Sheila."

As the island came into sight the captain told us, "This is the island. You have to get out here quickly." We hurriedly got out of the boat, one after the other. The shore was lined with high rocks and it was difficult for the women and children to climb over them. Muthana and I each picked up a child and carried them on our shoulders. After we came to the smaller rocks, we realized we were on one large rock or a small outcropping in the middle of the sea. The shore of the Greek island of Mytilene was 500 meters away. The captain had tricked us. I think he had left us there hoping to get away quickly so he would not be seen by the authorities. We were shocked and frightened and did not know how we were going to get to safety. It was eleven o'clock at night, our clothes were soaking, and we were very cold. The captain pointed to the shore and said, "That's Mytilene." It was too far to swim, especially for the children and their families. We were stranded.

I was forced to call Sheila. My phone was still with me and had some network coverage. I told her where the rock was, and the name of the island, and she looked for our location on the internet so she could inform the refugee commission. She contacted their office in Athens while some of us called the smuggler to tell him what had happened. The smuggler called the Greek coastguard and told them to look for us. We lay flat on the ground so nobody could see us because we were afraid, since we knew that it was the job of the coastguard to detain refugees and take their fingerprints, possibly sending us back to Iraq.

The captain then showed up! The motor had stalled again, and he had been unable to leave the outcropping. He begged us, "If we are arrested by the Greek police don't tell them about me because if they find out they'll put me in prison for at least seven years!" Some of the refugees helped the captain to slash and hide the rubber boat.

After some time searching for us, the coastguard silently came up to us and trained their lights on us. There was an officer and several soldiers. I heard the officer asking, "Does any one of you speak English?" I was afraid to tell him that I spoke a little so remained silent. Nobody answered him. Then he asked, "Where is the captain who brought you here?" He repeated this several times, but no one answered him. This made him angry and he began to fire his gun in the air. He then began to hit and kick us. Muthana was kicked in the stomach and the pain made him let out a sound which made me laugh nervously. We were very frightened, faced with an unknown fate. Finally, an Iraqi man got up and pointed towards the captain. The coastguard went over to him and dragged him out from among us, kicking him viciously and beating him while he wept and begged God for help. They bound his hands and took him with them. A short time after that, the officer apologized for this treatment of us. He then told us they would take us one by one to their ship via a small boat which could only take four people at a time. Then he started asking us questions, "Where have you come from?" All the Iraqis said, "We are Palestinians" out of fear of being returned to Iraq. The Iraqis have a country to be sent back to, but the Palestinians are stateless and so cannot be sent back.

Once we had all boarded the big ship, they photographed us sitting there and again began to kick and punch the captain. I was angry at their inhumane behavior. When we arrived at the harbor a Greek officer was there sitting on a chair with a table in front of him, taking our names and fingerprints. He then sent us to one of the hospitals for chest X-rays as they were worried that we might be carrying contagious diseases. After the medical examinations ended at 3 am, we were put in a temporary camp for refugees. Everyone was given a bed. There was a huge number of people in that camp from all different nationalities: Afghans, Iraqis and Palestinians. There was a separate section for women and children.

That night while I was sleeping, I dreamed of a white-walled house surrounded by orange trees. I was riding a horse in a field beside the house. When I woke up, I felt that it was telling me something good about the future. I wanted to call Sheila and tell her. That morning I familiarized myself with the way of life in the camp and learned what I should do. Then I bought a new phone to call Sheila. I told her about the dream and that I felt it was a vision of my future.

We experienced some suffering in that camp. We were not permitted to go out and feel the breeze or see the sun. I was in contact with someone from Amnesty International called Saeed. He was familiar with everything we had experienced and wrote a detailed report on our situation. He promised me that he would take our case to the refugee commission in Athens. After a few days, thankfully we were all released, and I was visited by a Greek lawyer named Agaliki. I gave her a follow-up statement about my case. Sheila was also in contact with her. This service was free, as the lawyer was working for the refugee commission. When we left the camp each of us was given a legal document called a *Khartee* in Greek that stated we had temporary residence. It allowed us to travel around and to leave for up to a month. Now we were able to book ferry tickets to travel to mainland Greece, which was 13 hours away.

I said goodbye to the people who left, but I stayed in Mytilene to complete my application for asylum. While looking for a hotel I met two Palestinians I knew. They were working as smugglers. We greeted each other and I told them I was looking for a hotel. They told me to come with them and we went into a Greek neighborhood. As I was walking, I saw a hotel called the New Life Hotel, at the end of a long street. It had white walls and was surrounded by orange trees, just like the house I had seen in my dream! I stayed in that hotel alone for a month and got to know the owner. I even developed a liking for Greek music. I submitted the asylum papers to the Greek police. When I went to the police station, I saw the same policeman who had taken my fingerprints when we arrived on that island!

Sheila and me in Athens, Greece 2007

During this time, I was in constant contact with my family and with Sheila. Waiting for a response from the Greek police, I was in a heightened emotional state filled with anticipation. I spent my days wandering around looking at the buildings and the shops and the sea. Then I received terrible news from my family. My brother Tarik had sold the flat in Baghdad and traveled to Turkey and then to Greece, where he had been kidnapped by a Kurdish gang. They had taken him to an unknown location in Athens and were demanding a ransom. I called my brother and he told me that he was not in good health. I decided to go to Athens and rescue my brother from the clutches of the gang before he came to serious harm.

I took the 13-hour journey by ferry and when I arrived, I met some Palestinians I knew including my friend Muthana. I asked them for help finding a hotel and began calling Tarik. He told me that the gang wanted a ransom of $3000 before they set him free. I contacted them to convince them that I did not have this money. I told them that I could only give them $1500 and I would borrow the rest from friends. The gang agreed to this. I called them to make the arrangements and told them that I would not give them the money until Tarik was set free. They agreed to this and we stayed in contact. My phone was always on so I could follow their directions. They gave me an address and I entered a small alleyway. They were watching me the whole time. They told me to stop and I saw a car pull up at the top of the street. My brother got out and headed toward me. I gave them the money and they left. Tarik and I embraced. He tried to kiss my hand, but I wouldn't let him. We went to the hotel where I was staying.

I left my brother and returned to Mytilene where I waited for a reply about my asylum application. None came. Sheila decided to come to Greece to apply for a fiancé visa at the American embassy in Athens. She bought a ticket to Mytilene. It was October of 2007. I bought the most beautiful bunch of flowers I could find and went to meet her at the airport. I was longing to see her. I didn't know how I would feel after this long period of suffering, pain and exile. The truth is I can't describe how I felt. I stood there waiting and she came through the arrival doors dressed in the traditional Palestinian dress I had bought her when I was in Syria in 2006. That was the last time we had been together. I could see from her face that she was exhausted from the journey. We embraced and wept, and I held her tightly to my chest. I had so longed to see her during the harsh and painful times I had been through. Early the next day we bought tickets and took the 13-hour ferry ride to Athens so we could go to the U.S. Embassy to apply for a fiancé visa. The waves were high, and the ship was rocking back and forth for the whole trip.

After arriving in Athens, we went to the American embassy, but they would not let us enter. We made an appointment and went again. This time they gave us a fiancé visa application form to complete, which we did. We then had an appointment with an American consul official who was very short with us. She seemed annoyed with Sheila for wanting to marry a refugee and, because I had been arrested by the Syrian intelligence agency, she demanded we bring a document from the Syrian government stating that there were no charges against me. Sheila and I went to the Syrian embassy in Athens and explained the situation to an official there. When we asked for this document so we could give it to the American embassy he laughed at us. "That's impossible," he said, "You want me to give you papers for the American embassy? Are you crazy?" He didn't give us the papers because I was not Syrian, and they gave papers only to Syrian citizens.

Sheila and I had breakfast in the hotel each morning and got to know the owner. Not knowing our plans, she at one point said to me, "It's impossible to get a visa to America or to go there." We didn't say anything.

The American Embassy also required that I get a stamp on my travel document from the Iraqi embassy because I did not have a birth certificate. We waited a long time at the Iraqi embassy information desk. When my turn came, I told them about my situation, explaining that I wanted them to verify or stamp my travel document, but they would not do this and again we left disappointed. I felt all the doors were shutting in our faces. As Sheila and I sat and looked at the night sky and the moon I said, "If only we lived up there on the moon, just me and you, away from the noise and problems of human beings. There would be just love, peace and safety…"

Sheila's vacation ended, and the time came for her to return to America. She was determined, however, to complete the application process from there. I also did my part by obtaining a legal passport from the Palestinian Authority, which would be accepted by the U.S. if ever we succeeded in obtaining a visa. Sheila had gotten the addresses of ten lawyers in Syria who were well-respected. However, when she called them and explained that we needed a non-conviction certificate they quickly said that unfortunately they could not help and hung up the phone. Whenever she mentioned the name of the prison – Far' Filistin – they were afraid because this was a known political prison. But finally, she reached a lawyer who promised to help. He was able to obtain a certificate from the Syrian authorities that confirmed there were no charges against me. Sheila paid his $500 fee and then had the document translated into English.

I don't remember how we were able to waive the requirement for a birth certificate. Sheila had collected all the possible documents from my past, including prior travel documents, identity cards, and whatnot. I believe that the American embassy eventually accepted one of my old identity cards instead of a birth certificate. Finally, we submitted the complete application and all the required documentation.

Another appointment was made for me at the American Embassy in Greece for March 2008. To avoid the long journey back and forth from Mytilene, I suggested to Sheila that I rent a flat in Athens to live in until it was time for the meeting. I tried to look for work but unfortunately, I couldn't find anything because of not speaking the language and the poor economic situation in Greece. Someone I knew offered me work in his business of smuggling but I refused. This man had been one of the strongest people opposed to my leaving Baghdad. Besides, I did not want to do anything illegal and risk my entire future.

Muthana and I rented a flat along with a new friend, Ahmed. The flat was owned by a Greek lady and was on the ground floor in an area called Attiki. We gradually furnished the flat by gathering things from the street. Once, we found a fridge in the street and pulled it all the way to our house on a cart. We were happy to find it worked well. We also came across a television and bought a satellite dish to go with it. I invited my brother Tarik to live with us before he went to one of the Scandinavian countries. He had twice tried to get there through the airport but had not succeeded. Some other people also came to live with us before traveling to European countries. We got to know them and listened to their stories. Many of them had no money so we let them stay with us for free as we were all refugees and shared the same ordeal.

After a wait of almost five months in Athens, it was time for my appointment at the American embassy. I bought new clothes and shoes to wear for the meeting. I arrived at the embassy, took a ticket, and waited for my turn. This time I felt the same American consul was relaxed and happy to see me again. I later learned that through Sheila's efforts, Senator Edward Kennedy had made efforts to speed up my case. In addition to this, through Sheila's advocacy, I had received letters of recommendation from Sheila's father (who is a retired colonel in the U.S. Army), Amnesty International, and one of Sheila's colleagues named Justin, who worked for the U.N. in Iraq. These letters of support were a lot of help in pushing my case forward.

At the end of the meeting with the consul and an interpreter from Lebanon named Joyce, the consul decided to grant me a fiancé visa to travel to America. She explained that my current passport from the Palestinian Authority had to remain in the embassy until the next day so it could be stamped. I said that was fine and thanked her profusely. I was so happy that when I left the building I was laughing and dancing in the street. I quickly called Sheila and gave her the news. She was ecstatic.

But the next day I got a call from the embassy. It was from Joyce, the interpreter. "Unfortunately, we have to tell you that your visa has been delayed. It may take a week, two weeks or perhaps longer." Apparently, the visa would not print because my name had triggered an alarm in the FBI database.

Sheila and I were plunged into despair. She called Senator Edward Kennedy's office and reported what happened. His immigration expert, a very kind woman named Emily, told Sheila that if any part of a name was similar to the name of a terrorist, it could create a "match" on the FBI database, and all of the relevant cases would have to be reviewed. Since my full name is "Thaer Shafiq Ali Abdallah," it is no wonder that the database was triggered! How many "Ali's" are there in the world? Emily told Sheila that such complications can take "months to years" to work out. She had Senator Kennedy request expedited review of my case.

To complicate matters further, I received notice that my asylum application in Greece had been denied, and I had four weeks to leave the country.

I counted down the weeks. The first week passed, then the second, then the third. The fourth week began, and I began to feel so nervous I had pains in my chest and heart. When Sheila called me, she could tell from the changed tone of my voice how exhausted I was. She told her father and he called me to give some reassurance and calm my fears. The next day Joyce called me. She greeted me with "Thaer, I have some news for you. You've got the visa!"

"Are you sure?" I asked. I was so happy I could barely believe what she was saying. The next day I went to the American Embassy accompanied by my friend Ahmed. They gave me my passport and the visa with its American stamp. Then I returned home. I was afraid to tell anyone else I had the visa, so I kept the news to myself. But of course, I called Sheila and told her the news. She was extremely happy and arranged to come to Athens in a week's time to take me back to America with her. After

The VISA I have worked so hard for

everything that had happened, she didn't trust matters to work out if I traveled on my own. I began to pack in complete secrecy and silence. I told my friends I was going to live in Mytilene and that they would have to pay all the rent after a month. I felt that I had to hide my news from them, as I didn't want anyone to spoil things for me and to steal the joy I felt about seeing Sheila. However, I did decide to tell my brother Tarik. He was leaving for Italy and planning to go to Norway to live. I wanted to raise his spirits. Before he left for the airport, I showed him my passport. He couldn't take in what he was seeing. "What is this?" he said amazed.

"I got the visa and I'm going to America." He was very happy for me. Two days later, he left and made his way safely to Norway.

Sheila arrived in Greece and we had less than 24 hours in Athens before it was time to travel to America. I said goodbye to my friends and told them I was going to Mytilene.

When we entered the Athens airport the officials there stopped me for half an hour because they had never seen a Palestinian passport with an American visa. Although we showed them the special American embassy envelope it came in, they still spent some time investigating me. Thank God that Sheila was with me and was able to explain everything to the officials. After getting through these complications and obstacles, we boarded the plane. I couldn't believe that I could finally relax a bit.

The plane took off and began the ten-hour journey from Greece to America. We landed in New York City. But something strange happened to me just as the plane's wheels touched the earth. The moment I finally reached my destination, I was suddenly struck by a terrible sense of exile and of being far away from home. I felt as though I was weeping inside. How could I live in America? I felt like a tree whose roots had been torn out. How could I be planted in another place? How could I live in the country that had occupied Iraq?

# CHAPTER ELEVEN
# My Arrival in America: 2008

I entered the United States of America in New York City on Sunday, April 13, 2008. I took my first steps slowly in this land, gazing with amazement at everything from the vast airport to the American police officers in their uniforms. I said to myself, "I've never seen anything like this outside of American movies." When I approached the counter, the Passport Control officer took my passport and gestured with his hand toward a room as he returned it to me. Sheila and I went into this room and handed our passports to the officer who said, in English, "Have a seat." "What does that mean?" I asked Sheila. "It means *taffadul al jalous*, 'please sit.'" This was new to me. I had previously only known "siddown!"

We waited for a long time. My patience began to fade, and a fire started to burn inside of me from anxiety and thinking of all the bad things that might happen. We both knew that I could be denied entrance, even at this, the very last moment. We waited for fifteen minutes or more and my anxiety and tension grew and grew. After a grueling 10 hours on the plane we were exhausted. After twenty minutes, I was burning with anxiety. I said to myself, "Oh my God I don't want any more problems and I don't want to be detained again. I've given them everything they asked of me." To keep our fears at bay, Sheila and I began singing. It was a childhood song that Sheila's parents had taught her, and I had learned from Sheila. "I love you, a bushel and a peck, a bushel and a peck and a hug around the neck." We repeated this song over and over for thirty minutes. It felt like three years. I could see the officer from a distance and said to myself, "When is he going to pick up my passport, stamp it and give it back to me?" Suddenly, he picked it up and began doing checks on the computer. He stamped it then called me by name. We hastened toward him.

"What now?" I asked anxiously. "You can go now," he said. We couldn't believe it! Thank God! We passed through the rest of the routine checks in the airport without difficulty. After reclaiming our luggage, we headed toward the arrival hall. Sheila's father Paul was waiting for us outside and we hurried toward him. We were dying to see him and we both threw our arms around him and kissed him. (He had given us a letter to use if we came across any problems in the airport that said to contact him. He was a retired colonel and had been in the army at the time when military service was compulsory in America. Luckily, he had not taken part in any wars.) As we embraced, he said to me, "Didn't I tell you that we would have a beer together in Boston? Remember when I said that to you in Syria in 2006?"

I said, "Yes, I remember. I remember it well."

We headed for Sheila's father's car, a red nineteen-nineties Volkswagen, all of us deliriously happy. We then set off on the four-hour journey from New York to their home in Boston, MA. Our faces were etched with tiredness as we arrived in their small, quiet town of Walpole. We were greeted by Sheila's mother Mary Ellen who was so eager to see us she ran out to meet us in her bare feet. "Finally, you're here!" she said, embracing me. "I couldn't feel safe until this moment!"

We went into the house where Sheila's mother had been watching an American baseball game with the team that she loved called the Boston Red Sox, something I knew nothing about as I was still new in the country. I didn't even know English at that point. Sheila's parents welcomed me warmly into their home. Her mother had been shopping at a Lebanese supermarket and bought stuffed grape leaves and tabbouleh that she prepared for us to eat. Afterwards we went upstairs to a room with green walls which emanated a sense of comfort and peace. Here, exhausted by the long journey, I lay down and fell into a deep sleep.

When I awoke, at first I didn't know where I was. Then I decided to call my sisters in Jordan and Iraq to let them know where I was. They didn't even know that I had gotten the visa! When I told my sister Bushra she was very happy and said, "Forget Iraq. Don't think about it at all. Think about the future and forget Baghdad. Just forget it." I called my sister Manal in Jordan and she was so happy to hear the good news she cried. Because I had arrived safely in America, she gave out sweets to her neighbors. Whenever I think about this my eyes fill with tears.

Early that day we ate breakfast and then agreed to go for lunch at a restaurant where I met Sheila's sister Ellen and her brother David. After spending several good days at Sheila's father's house, I then went to stay in Sheila's place which was a one-room studio flat in Somerville, MA. Paul came along to help me move in. It was a single room, with a refrigerator and a hot plate instead of a kitchen. This was Sheila's place while she was taking premedical studies. She also worked as a secretary at Massachusetts General Hospital from 3 pm to 11:30 pm and went to and from work by bicycle.

There was a condition attached to giving me the visa and allowing me to enter the USA. If Sheila and I did not get married within three months I would have to leave America and go back to where I came from! But Sheila, as always, was prepared. She had already arranged for us to get officially married legally very quickly. We got married in a mosque in Wayland, MA on April 21, 2008 where we signed our marriage contract in the Islamic way, witnessed by the Imam Talal Eid. Sheila's family attended as well as the Imam's wife and children. Before the marriage ceremony I prayed two prostrations in supplication to God to ask for guidance.

I began to organize my new life. Sheila and her father enrolled me in a program at the YMCA so I could learn English. The next day Paul and I took the subway to the Huntington YMCA where I was going to study. I did not know much English at all, and I felt very embarrassed. After entering the tall building, we paid $400 for the four-month course. When we left, Sheila's father and I began to feel hungry, so we looked for somewhere to eat. As we were standing outside, Paul saw a restaurant with a sign saying "Boston Shawarma." "That is definitely an Arab restaurant!" I said.

We went inside. The owner, Fayez, was talking on the phone. I felt immediately happy! He had an Iraqi accent and it was the first time I had heard one since arriving in America. After he finished his call, I greeted him in Arabic, and he responded. I introduced myself and Sheila's father. I told him that I had only arrived in America and Boston a week ago and had just registered at the YMCA across the street from his restaurant. He welcomed me warmly in the cheerful way Iraqis receive their guests. After we ate, I got out the money to pay Fayez, but he refused to take it, saying, "No, absolutely not, it is not our way to take money from guests." I was very happy and said to myself, "It's as if we are in Iraq. The Iraqis haven't changed. They still keep their customs and character here in America." I thanked him enthusiastically and wished him well.

After I returned to Sheila's home and her father headed to his, I started to feel how much I missed and longed for my family and friends and the life I had in Iraq. I especially missed my mother. I spent forty days dreaming about all the things that had happened to me in Iraq and all the places I had lived there. One day I saw a photograph of a woman and was struck with how much she resembled my mother. It occurred to me to paint her picture, so I bought some paints, brushes and canvas. There was not much space to paint in the narrow studio apartment, but I sat in a corner and managed as best as I could. As I painted, I saw my mother in my mind. I missed her so much I would have given anything to see her in person, if only for a minute. I poured all my creative energy into that picture which was the first one I painted in Boston. It remains unlike any other work I have done, because it contains a piece of my heart.

My sense of exile and homesickness grew, and the feeling of intensely missing my friends and family was slowly killing me. I didn't know anyone in Boston. I didn't speak English well so I didn't know who I could talk to. I began to feel as though I was losing the traditions and customs I had inherited from my family and that everything was changing. I still spoke with my sisters over the phone, and Sheila did not neglect me. She tried to fill me with happiness, and helped me to become familiar with the neighborhood, but those first months in Boston were miserable for me. In order to fill the void of loneliness I felt inside, I also decided to find a job. Once I had obtained permission, I began working with Sheila's brother David who had a business repairing boats. He taught me how to paint the bottom of the boats and spoke to me in English the whole time. I learned a new word whenever David asked me to bring him something and I quickly wrote them down in a little notebook so I wouldn't forget them. Unfortunately, the company eventually closed, because of the deterioration in the American economy due to the 2008 financial crisis. I personally feel that this crisis was made worse by the massive amount of money spent on the wars the country had embarked upon.

Sheila and I stayed four months in the studio apartment and afterwards moved to a new place with a bedroom, sitting room and a balcony. It really was much better than the old place in Somerville. We moved our things in with the help of Sheila's father and arranged them to suit the new apartment. Fortunately, it was near the Forest Hills train station where we could take the orange line into downtown Boston. One day when I was going to the train, I met a Moroccan man named Hassan who had a small kiosk in the station. He was a very kind and decent person and when he learned that I was new in the country he helped me a lot. He gave me free phone cards to call my family. Our friendship grew to the point where I would look out for him every time I took the train downtown to my English class, but the feelings of homesickness and loneliness still followed me.

I started taking the subway to the YMCA every day. It was very far from our apartment so every evening I would return home exhausted. I wasn't managing well to divide my time between the classes and homework, and thoughts of my family never left my mind.

I decided to occupy myself with anything else I could find, and asked Sheila to teach me how to use the computer. This was something I had never learned, as it was forbidden in Iraq! She began to teach me, and I wrote down everything she told me. To keep boredom at bay I also headed to the kitchen and began learning how to cook. For this I sought the advice of my sisters over the phone. Every Sunday my sister Khitam would call me from Norway and talk for hours as the calls were free. During these conversations, she told me how to cook Palestinian and Iraqi dishes and I would write down her instructions in my notebook which I have kept to this day. I also learned the English alphabet from scratch. Each time I learned a new letter or word I stuck it to the wall on a piece of paper, but this began to annoy Sheila, as there were bits of paper stuck all over the apartment!

However, soon we had another happy occasion that took my mind off homesickness. Sheila had been preparing all along to have a larger wedding ceremony, and so after a few months of moving into and organizing the new apartment, Sheila and I celebrated a blessing of our marriage at St. Catherine of Siena Catholic Church in Norwood. There were more than one hundred guests, mostly Sheila's American friends and family. But by then I had made some American friends as well who are still close to my heart, including Bob Cable and his wife, Lorraine, Donna Perry, and Dorothy Buck and her husband, Anselm Blumer.

The ceremony was conducted by Brian Pierce, a Dominican friar, and Imam Talal Eid, who had performed our Islamic marriage. Each of us entered the marriage according to our respective religions: Sheila in the Christian way and me in the Muslim way. It was the first time this church had witnessed an interfaith marriage with this degree of love and acceptance, with a priest and a Muslim imam leading the service together. In front of everyone, I prayed in Arabic, and Sheila translated my words into English. Afterwards we went to a nearby banquet hall for the wedding reception. It was arranged in the American tradition, but to make sure I didn't feel alone and far from my family, Sheila had put up pictures of them on a poster board. That way, I could feel as if they were with us.

Fr. Brian Pierce, OP and Imam Dr. Talal Eid

The church where Sheila and I got married

After we ate dinner and cut the wedding cake, we put on the music and danced our first dance to the well-known song "Hello" by Lionel Ritchie. Sheila and I had often sung this song to each other when we were in the desert refugee camps. As we danced together, I looked into her beautiful blue eyes and I felt as though her spirit was emanating from her like a white dove flying up to the sky.

We spent our honeymoon in a historic town called Plymouth where Sheila's parents had a summerhouse, a quiet place near the ocean. After a week, we returned to our apartment and my working life began. I started to teach Arabic to our friend Dorothy and she in turn taught me English. I also spent a year taking English lessons with one of the charities in downtown Boston called the International Institute of Boston. At first, I met one of the teachers whose name was David (I noticed that a lot of Americans had this name) and he carried out an assessment of my language skills. I felt ashamed at not being able to speak English and I was still dogged with homesickness and loneliness.

David placed me in Class 1, but as I improved I moved up to Class 2, then 3 and then 4. The teachers were very good, kind people. I remember them all well. Deborah, God rest her soul, was a very thoughtful teacher who sadly died of cancer, and Ellen, a Jewish teacher was always cheerful and friendly with the students and taught in such a way that it was easy for us to understand her lessons. There was also a teacher named Shireen, another teacher from China whose name I don't remember, the head of the organization whose name was Jude and her assistant Emily.

While studying English at the institute I made friends with people from many different backgrounds and nationalities. There were additional subjects available for refugees such as the preparation for the written portion of the driving test to get one's driver's license. I also joined an evening class near our apartment in Jamaica Plain to get some extra English lessons and after that I felt that I was finally making progress in my mind and in my life. As I gradually learned English my sense of shame began to fade but I still wanted to learn more and more.

At a Palestinian community center, I met a man named Yusuf and his brother Naser. I worked with them in a pizza restaurant for a bit and during this time Yusuf gave me a great piece of advice: get a piece of chalk and write all my goals and ambitions for the year on the wall. I did this and found that indeed every year I achieved something new from my list of life goals. The most important one of these was achieving my dream of learning to drive. First, I took classes for the driver's written test and obtained my learner's permit, then Paul helped me learn by giving me driving lessons in his red 1999 VW. Accompanied by my Iraqi friend Fayez, I took the test in Chinatown and I passed.

By this time, Sheila was in medical school. She had a school vacation and she and I decided to go to Chicago to visit some Palestinian families who had come to American as refugees from the Al-Waleed camp on the Iraqi border. It was a fifteen-hour drive to Chicago from Boston. I was very happy to drive on the highway for the first time! Our first stop was to visit the family of Abu Osama, a friend who was also like a father to me. I also visited my great friends Qusay (who had helped me in the camp!), Abu Khaled, and Omar Mohammed Abd Al-Hadi, known as Omar Jambo. We enjoyed their warm welcome and hospitality for a week. It was amazing to see these people again, and to marvel that we had come all the way from the desert camps now to an American city.

When we returned to Boston, I decided to enroll for classes in the Eliot School of Fine and Applied Arts, which was near our apartment. My teacher there was impressed by my work and offered to arrange an exhibition of my paintings. I was delighted by this development. The exhibition – my first in America - was held at a Lebanese restaurant called The Middle East, through the Out of the Blue gallery in Jamaica Plain, MA. Sheila helped me prepare for it and advertise it. Many of our friends attended, and in one hour I sold six paintings! I have never since sold so many paintings in just one showing.

I began to learn a lot from Americans. I met a friend named Michael who was from a Polish Jewish background. After hearing my story, he encouraged me to write a book about my life. From time to time I was invited to give exhibitions and lectures in various places. I also got to know the Arabic speaking community in Boston and through them met another Thaer, a Palestinian who had lived in America for a long time. He had a chain of shops called BD's and gave me a studio for free in the basement of one of his stores, so I could devote myself to my art. In my exile, I felt I had found a brother in him. He supported me and was very kind to me in ways I will never forget. I hope to be able to do the same for him one day. The best thing about the studio he gave me was that it was near our apartment. I met several people in this area including Thaer's brother Tawfiq, Abu Eid, Nasser, Ziad and Abd Al-Hafeez. I completed many paintings in this studio and was invited to exhibit my work and give talks about my life. I gave around fifteen of these talks. This was all thanks to Sheila's support and help in arranging the details of the exhibitions and lectures. Her parents also played a huge role by giving me constant encouragement.

A photo of Thaer Tufaha and me in front of one of his BD's Discount stores
located in Chelsea MA.

The first talk I gave was at Massachusetts General Hospital. This was arranged with the help of Sheila's friend Donna Perry who worked there as a nurse. She was a lovely person who has also done a lot of work and research on Palestinian human rights. I began to get more invitations from churches, universities, and social and humanitarian organizations. At the same time, I was looking for work. I submitted more than thirty applications and attended many interviews but due to the recession I did not find anything.

I continued to paint. I had initially painted pictures of refugee life, and traditional Arab figures. But as I started to notice that America had a lot of poverty and suffering as well, I started to paint American subjects. In our neighborhood, I got to know two homeless people, Joe and Steve, who were from Polish backgrounds. Steve used to sleep under our balcony and at night made loud screaming noises that stopped me from sleeping. When I tried to help him, I got to know him, and l learned that he was a former postman and an intelligent, peace-loving man. He also knew a lot about Palestine, always wore a Palestinian *Keffiya,* a head covering, and often took part in demonstrations against the Israeli occupation. I decided to paint Steve and Joe's portraits, so I took photographs of them, then made oil paintings. We became friends during the time we lived in that apartment.

To make my status in America permanent, I applied for a Green Card with the help of Madeleine Choi Cronin, a lawyer who helped me to correctly prepare my file. Sheila had gone to her about my case and she had kindly refused to take any money for the work she did for me. We couldn't thank her enough.

I worked for four months at a candy-making company called Dancing Deer, then finally found a permanent job. This was thanks to someone named Marvin Traub, a well-known businessman who had been the CEO of Bloomingdales department stores. He and his wife Lee fund scholarships for Harvard students, and years ago when Sheila was an undergraduate at Harvard, she was a "Traub scholar." Every year he and his wife came from New York to Boston to take the current and former Traub scholars to dinner at Harvard Square. In 2009, I went with Sheila and met both of them and they were very welcoming and kind. They already knew all about me, because when I was in prison in Syria their son, who was a journalist, had tried to help me. When I met Mr. Traub in person, I asked him if I could work at Bloomingdales at an entry-level position. He asked me to email him my CV, which I did. Within a week, someone from Bloomingdales called and invited me to come to Bloomingdales in Chestnut Hill for a job interview. Accompanied by my friend Sameer, I went and took various tests and assessments. Sameer translated for me so I could understand the instructions and rules on the computer. I began working for Bloomingdale's in the women's shoe department. The work was part time, only when they needed me. One of my colleagues was a Cuban woman called Michelle who became, and still is, a very dear friend of mine. I worked in different departments including carpets, furnishings and in the warehouse and got to know many of the employees there who were all very good to me. I met the secretary and the manager, Joanne, who was Lebanese and we spoke a few words together in Arabic. They were all very kind and treated me well. I never felt that I experienced any racism or discrimination. But I didn't like the work because it was not constant. It was only sporadic, and the wages were low.

However, I kept at it, and I eventually found a full-time job within Bloomingdales. It was as a dishwasher and cleaner in a restaurant within the store called Forty Carrots. I was there for about a year. The manager, Yasin, was goodhearted and easy to work with. One of my colleagues however was an older man from Mexico who often troubled me with his racism. He often hurt my feelings to the point where I decided to leave and look for another job. My friend and neighbor Rodrigo helped me with this. Rodrigo was from Latin America and lived in the apartment above us with his American wife Carly, a medical student. I told him I was looking for work and he took me with him to a company where I met a woman called Saria and filled in an application form. When I was accepted, I started working with him as a janitor at Curry College where I worked from nine o'clock in the evening until two o'clock in the morning. One of the buildings was an art building. As I wandered through the rooms and corridors looking at the paints and brushes and stands, I longed to study art. I asked Professor Lorrie Alberto, one of the art teachers, if I could exhibit my work there and give a talk. Once we discussed this, she agreed that I could arrange the exhibition and give a talk about my life. It was a wonderful event, and Curry College awarded me its 2012 Human Rights Award.

Soon afterwards, after three years of marriage, we found out that Sheila was pregnant! Every night I would stroke her abdomen and pray for her. She began her medical visits and check-ups and we both attended the ultrasound scan. When I saw the baby's movements and heard the heartbeat, my own heart skipped a beat. I felt sure it was a boy. And yes -- Yusef was born on June 18, 2011 at Brigham and Women's Hospital in Boston. It was permitted for the father to be present at the birth, so I was there with Sheila the whole time. When Yusef was born, crying and screaming and wriggling like a living doll, I was ecstatic. While they cleaned him and made sure he was doing well, I asked the doctor if I could whisper the call to prayer in his ear, as is the Islamic custom. As I did this, he stopped crying and raised his head and looked at me with his beautiful eyes. I felt he was speaking to me, telling me he knew the sound. I began to shake, and I had to bend over, weeping with happiness. I thanked God for the blessing he had bestowed on me in this beautiful child, my own son who would carry my name and help me to fill the terrible void of exile I felt from being so far from my family.

Me working overnight at Curry College with my friend Rodrigo

The night I won the Human Rights Award in 2012 at Curry College

The beginning of Yusef's life brought new life and new hope to me. He gave me incredible energy despite not letting me sleep! His grandparents Mary Ellen and Paul Provencher came to visit, delighted by the birth of their first grandchild. It was the best gift we could ever give them. We moved to our third apartment which was on Rossmore Road in Jamaica Plain. We took a bigger place with three bedrooms, so my mother could come and live with us. At this time, I took a citizenship course at the Irish International Immigrant Center, taught by a wonderful teacher named Diana.

The day Yusef was born on June 18TH 2011

My wife Sheila, my son Yusef and me a few days after he was born

My Mother-in-law Mary Ellen and Father-in-law Paul Provencher holding my son Yusef. Their first grandchild.

Yusef at 5 months old

Within the same month in 2012, Yusef turned one year old, Sheila graduated from Harvard Medical School and became a doctor, and I became an American citizen! What a year! I immediately applied for my mother to immigrate to the United States. After two years of efforts and with the help of the Irish International Immigrant Center, we managed to get a family reunion visa for my mother, and she came to America. I went to get her in Turkey and accompanied her to the United States, just as Sheila had accompanied me years before.

My mother was greeted on her arrival by Paul and Mary Ellen, my wife Sheila and our son Yusef whom she saw for the first time at age three. Her coming gave me renewed hope and energy. Life had had no flavor for me while she was so far away.

We took my mother to lots of places in Boston and introduced her to many Iraqi, Palestinian, and American families. The Irish International Immigrant Center in Boston threw a party to welcome all immigrants, and I took this opportunity to thank everyone who had helped me and my mother come to America, such as the lawyer Abby Colbert, who had prepared my mother's case for free, and Kate in U.S. Representative Michael Capuano's office.

My mother and I

A photo of my father in the early 1980's

A pic of me and my friend Ronnie Millar, the Director of the Irish International
Immigrant Center

My mother had only nine joyful months with us at our apartment in Chelsea, MA when she suffered a stroke which caused acute bleeding in her brain. She passed away, God rest her soul. I grieved deeply at her loss. How I wished she could have remained alive and lived with us until the end of time. However, nothing lasts forever, and fate is the master of us all. There is no way to trick our destiny. Many friends attended her funeral at the Islamic Society of Boston mosque in Roxbury, MA and she was prayed for by Muslims, Jews and Christians. She was buried in a Boston cemetery. The shock of her death affected me for two years. I couldn't handle it. I still miss her and think of the beautiful times we spent together. She had become a friend as well as a mother and we were all, including my son Yusef, deeply attached to her. She had filled my childhood with love and tenderness and had always been there for me in my times of crisis. The American community in Boston had known her and loved her. In her honor, I collected her memories in a book about her experiences entitled, "No Place to Call Home: My Life as a Palestinian Refugee," that was translated into English.

In 2015, Sheila finished her medical residency and started working as a full-fledged family physician at a community health center in Lynn, MA. We moved to East Boston, where we had wonderful neighbors Peter and his wife Brendalee, and I dedicated my life to looking after the house and caring for Yusef. Every morning I took him to the school bus and then collected him in the afternoon. My son has gotten bigger and he is now nine years old. He learned Spanish at school and every Sunday he went to Arabic class. Yusef is becoming an artist in his own right -- he started painting at age 2, and I have saved many of his drawings and paintings. Also, I have started a band named Al-Sultan that plays music at Arabic weddings and celebrations. And to complete our joy, Sheila became pregnant again at age 44, and in November 2017 gave birth to our daughter Nora. Nora fills the house with energy and keeps us all on our toes!

In 2019, we finally left Boston to move into our own home in central Massachusetts. After starting out together in a tent in the desert, then a furnished room, then a one-bedroom apartment, then a series of two and three-bedroom apartments, at last Sheila and I were able to purchase a house with a yard for our children. We are beyond grateful for this chance, and are settling into our new community.

The United States is my home now. When I travel outside to see my family in Europe or the Middle East, my American passport brings me respect. But I have to say, when I come back to the airport in Boston or New York, especially after Donald Trump was elected president, the officers always make me step aside out of the line and they take me to another office and ask me many questions. Whenever this happens, I feel that America is *not* my home. I don't want this to happen to my children in the future and I hope the laws and practices change.

Now, in 2020, I continue to paint and live life with my family. I do not know what the future will bring. There is reason for fear and apprehension in the direction of global events. In fact, as I write this in early April 2020, we are living under stay-at-home orders due to the COVID-19 coronavirus global pandemic. The stores are all out of hand sanitizer, paper goods, and cleaning supplies. I am home taking care of the children and Sheila still goes out every day to work as a doctor. We do not know yet when or how this pandemic will end.

But in the moments in my home in the day-to-day routine, when I see my children, I am full of sincere thanks and appreciation for the blessings that have brought me to this life. I look forward to whatever is ahead.

The group I created in Boston named Al-Sultan

My beautiful family in 2018

My family at our new home in 2019

Nora all grown up in
2020

# POSTSCRIPT

I entitled this book 'Song in the Desert' because I do believe that each of our lives is a song . . . a unique work of art that is always changing, always being created. We create the music of our lives. When I finished this book, a project that took me 12 years, I shared it with one of my friends from Iraq. He responded by writing this poem to celebrate the unique story of my life. This poem, which is its own song, remains in its original music of Arabic. For this poem I am truly grateful, as I am grateful for the gift of my life.

–Thaer Abdallah, August 21, 2020

رحلة في ذاكرة الصديق

ثائر عبدالله


انسان وفنان
رمز الوفاء
فلسطيني الهوية والانتماء
عراقي الملامح والطباع
على جبينه طبع دجلة عناده

وأعتلى محياه شموخ نخيله

من عبق حارات القدس العتيقة

ارتشف عطره

من شجر زيتون فلسطين ارتوت جذوره

هو ثائر الحب والقضية

ثائر الفكر والانتماء

من جراحه لملم دوات حبره

ونحت من الصخر ريشته

رسم بشغف مئذنة قدسه

ومن حكايات جده طرز مفتاح بيته


يوم بكت سماء العراق مطرا اسود

وتكسرت صباحات بغداد غدرا

كانت خناجر ذوي القربى

تطعن كل بسمة

تمزق كل حياة

تذبح كل مقدس

كان عويل الموت

يجول في الطرقات

ينحر يسلب

ويهجر كل مهجر


مع اقتراب الموت المؤجل

والعبث بالحياة

قرر ذاك الموجوع قلبه

المفجوع بالشتات

الرحيل للمجهول

إلى أين ياثائر ؟

.. لا أدري

إلى الاغتراب

الى المنافي

إلى حيث خط لنا القدر

قدر الأجداد

كان المسير ثقيلا بين محطات الموت

الى أن حط بهم الترحال

على مرأى من الحدود الملعونة

وخطوط العار الذي مزق جسد الأمة

هناك دق أول وتد للخيام

في رمال الصحراء

وتد الإصرار على الحياة

على درب الرحيل الابدي


كان الطرق على الوتد

بمثابة صرخة مدوية بوجه

قاتلي الإنسانية المستباح

فكان الصبر وكان العطاء

كان لابد للأجساد أن تضج بالدماء

أجساد مزقتها اسلاك الوهم


كان ذلك الثائر

هو السباق هو المغامر

غرس قدميه في الرمال

عنادا حتى الذراع

كان البرد والصقيع

والقيض والربيع

كانت العواصف والأتربة

كان الخوف واليأس والجوع

كان الليل موحشا

حيث السباع والضباع

ليل كان اقرب إلفة من ذوي القربى

كان الوقت دهورا


ومع الصبر أثمر الدمع

مدت الإنسانية يدها

لتنفض غبار النار عن الخيام

خيام شاخت بعد أن هتك الريح ردائها

كاشفا مأساة كسر الانسان للأنسان

خيام تكورت تحتها هياكل

تحمل أسماء وجوه بلا ملامح

سوى من بريق خافت

لعيون تحكي ملحمة النكبة

وكأنها وديعة

من الأجداد إلى الأحفاد


مع فريق الأمل كان الأمل

يومها توقف الزمن امام ذلك الشاب

إمرأة مدت له بريق الحياة

أعادت نبض قلب شاخ قبل اوانه

قلب تكسر ألوانا بين الرمال

كانت الأنسانة شيلا هي البلسم

هي الحلم الجميل

حلم تسلل مع صباحات الندى

حلم ارتدى أناقة الغروب

حان وقت الوداع الأخير

طار معها على جناح ذلك الحب

في رحلة الحياة الموعودة

إلى ربوع بوسطن

هناك أثمر الوليد

بيتا سقفه الحنان

وصدى جدرانه معزوفة

غناء في الصحراء

وعلى أنغام ذلك الحب

كان أجمل لحن

لأجمل الأسماء

يوسف ونورا .

قبرص ١ حزيران ٢٠٢٠

ابو تغلب

Talal Al Hamdany Abo Taghlub

# ACKNOWLEDGEMENTS

God has compensated me for my exile by giving me friends and family in America. Before I came, all I knew about the community here was taken from the negative picture I had in my mind from experiencing the invasion by the U.S. army. After I arrived, my image of the USA changed entirely. I have made many American friends in Boston -- Jews, Muslims, Christians -- from many different nationalities. Many of them encouraged me to write my life story and I would like to express my gratitude to them.

First, a very special thanks to my wife Sheila who has stood by me faithfully and given her moral support throughout my many humanitarian struggles and legal challenges. To my children, Yusef and Nora, who both fill me with joy and gratitude every single day. Special thanks to dear Yusef who, at age 4 when we thought we didn't have enough money to produce this manuscript, lugged his piggybank full of change to me (the bank was actually shaped like a bear) and gave me all of his money to use to publish this book. Love and thanks to Paul Provencher, Sheila's father, who has been a friend, brother and father-in-law all in one. I also have enormous gratitude and respect for my mother-in-law Mary Ellen who has stood by me with love and compassion, especially after I lost my own mother. To my wife's sisters, Ellen, Maureen and Anne and her brother David who have all been very kind to me, to Laval Provencher, Paul's brother, who always likes to laugh with me, and to Laval's grandsons Matt and Al Johnson. Thanks also to Mary Ellen's brother John O'Brien who is always kind to me.

A special thanks to Adam Shapiro for trying to help me when I was in Syria and to Joyce Haley of the American Embassy in Athens for her help when she interviewed me and gave me the good news that my visa to America had been granted.

Thanks to the late Senator Edward Kennedy and his secretary Emily Winterson for fighting for a visa for me so I could enter the United States. Enormous thanks and appreciation to the lawyer Madeline Choi Cronin for helping me to get to America, to the lawyer Abby Colbert for helping me obtain American citizenship and for working on my mother's case, and to the lawyer Jenny who prepared my mother's file, all of whom offered their excellent skills and services for free. Thank you to Gladys for all the help she gave me in trying to fast-track my mother and sister's immigration cases and for helping many other Iraqi refugees, as well as to Katherine in Representative Michael Capuano's office who also tried to speed up the case.

Thanks to Sheila's cousins and their spouses, Adam and Denise Perrin, Christine and Amos Heckendorf and to Joan and Michelle Lamy, and to Peter and his wife Linda. Thanks also to her cousins Myanna and Christine Carbin-O'Brien, and to John O'Brien, Jr., a kind and soft-spoken man. Thank you to my mother-in-law's friends Mary Ann and Marilyn who have always encouraged me over the years.

Thanks to my dear "sister" Rana Awwad and her husband Imad Qasrawi. Rana was one of the first people to translate for me and has supported, encouraged and stood by me throughout my efforts to create this book. Thanks also to my brother Mohammed Al-Ghoul Al-Mansour Al-Harif for photographing me and my family for free.

Thank you to the International Institute of Boston organization for teaching me English and a special thanks and appreciation to my teacher Mrs. Ellen Courts, and to my kind teacher Susan Shernall. To my "big brother," Ronnie Millar, the director of the Irish International Immigrant Center who has stood by me and offered me cultural and moral support in so many ways, and to all the workers at the Irish International Immigrant Center (now the Rian Immigrant Center) for making me feel as though I had a second family in Boston. Thank you to Erik Jacobs, a photographer who contributed to the production of this book. A special thanks to Dr. Ramzi Nasir who was a great help to me when I was adjusting to life in America.

Thanks to my very dear friends, Bob Cable and his wife Lorraine, who have always been among the first to be supportive. Heartfelt thanks to my "brother" Thaer Tufaha, owner of the BD's shops, who has stood by me all this time and made me feel as though I was his younger brother. I will never forget how he offered me a free studio in which to paint. To my "brother," Yusuf Arzkat, for helping me find a home when I arrived in America and for encouraging me to achieve my goals. To the late Mr. Traub, the founder of Bloomingdale's, and his wife Lee for finding me a job when I arrived in America and for helping me write a book about my mother's life. Thanks to Joanne for her welcome and Laurie for her kindness and all the wonderful staff at Bloomingdale's.

Thank you to Donna Perry, whom I approached to ask if I could organize my first-ever talk about my life, in the hospital where she works. Special thanks to the team of artists including Vivienne Shalom, her sister Beverly Shalom, Phyllis Pullham and Adnan bin Ali, who is from Morocco. We have become like one family after expressing our message of peace and humanity through art. Thanks also to Rabbi Barbara who allowed me to give a talk on my mother's life in her synagogue in Boston and for the warm reception by those who attended the talk.

Thank you to the Al Hakim family, Bhaaldan and Fatin and their children Maryam, Fatima and Mohammed, all resettled in Worcester MA from Iraq. Fatin helped me study the history of barbering when I considered going to barber school. Thanks also to Ibrahim Zannouba and his wife Dahb Jolak, from Syria, with fond memories of their son Wael's wedding to Noor at the Tarbosh Restaurant in Worcester, where my band provided Arabic drums. Noor's father Nadim Shikh Omar and his wife Reem were always gracious and prepared delicious foods for us. Wael and Noor now have a baby boy named Ibrahim. Nadim's mother immigrated from Syria, and she reminds me of my own mother.

Thank you to Christine Shahadi Tawhim who continues to promote Arabic heritage in America, for teaching me about Arabic folklore and how to use the sword at weddings. To my friends Ben Kinawuz, Mr. Levi, Mr. Karim and Meghan Wyatt for their involvement and cooperation in establishing a heritage group, and to Mr. Jacob who helped set up websites for me and my mother. To Aziz Samir Abu Al- Saoud, and Nabih Al-Hakim, for encouraging my interview on his program, *Al Saa'a Al Arabi,* and to the sisters Janwa and Dima Hakim, who interviewed me and wonderfully described my mother. Thank you also to Ali Hakim, who made family photographs for us.

Thank you to Lauren who helped me when my mother was dying by sitting with us by her side and for filling out the hospital papers and sending them to the mosque, and to Michelle and her husband who brought us food in our grief.

I would also like to thank my friends Dietmar Ocasio and Jessenia Suarez for your help in completing my book. We have built a great friendship since we first met at MetroPCS in Chelsea MA. I appreciate the friendship we have built through the short time we have known each other.

Thank you also to my dear friends in East Boston including Yasser Munif and Elsa Wiehe and their children Yara and Zoya, and Karim and Elizabeth Tanefis and their children Majdouline and Telili. We had so many wonderful times and adventures taking our children to Arabic school together! Thanks to our next-door neighbors in East Boston, Peter and Brenda and their children, for bearing with our often-noisy family and rambunctious kids.

Thanks also to our new neighbors in Shrewsbury, MA especially Lisa and Stephen who have made us feel welcomed and at home.

I give my deepest and sincere gratitude for the support given me by the writer Samir Samara who became my friend after getting to know me through editing my story, and to Judy Barber in England for her help with translating the text along with Dorothy C. Buck who edited, organized and reviewed my book, and for the close friendship of Dorothy and her husband, Anselm in my exile.

Finally, to the one who keeps it all together, I love you Sheila.

*Thaer Abdallah*

119